ENCOUNTERING
BIGOTRY

ENCOUNTERING BIGOTRY

Befriending Projecting Persons in Everyday Life

Philip Lichtenberg
Janneke van Beusekom
Dorothy Gibbons

A GestaltPress Book
Cambridge, Massachusetts

A GestaltPress Book
66 Orchard Street, Cambridge MA 02140
gestaltpress@aol.com

Distributed by: **THE ANALYTIC PRESS**
                         101 West Street
                         Hillsdale, NJ 07642

Excerpts reprinted with the permission of Poseidon Press, a division of Simon & Schuster, from *Not By the Sword* by Kathryn Watterson. Copyright © 1995 by Kathryn Watterson. Excerpts reprinted with the permission of Routledge from *Teaching to Transgress: Education as the Practice of Freedom* by Bell Hooks. Copyright © 1994 Gloria Watkins. The authors express their gratitude to those whose names appear above for permission to use the passages indicated.

Library of Congress Cataloging-in-Publishing Data

Lichtenberg, Philip.
    Encountering bigotry: befriending projecting person in everyday life / Philip Lictenberg, Janneke van Beusekom, Dorothy Gibbons.
    Includes bibliographical references and index.
    ISBN 0-88163-384-4
    1. Toleration.   2. Prejudices.   3. Discrimination---Psychological aspects.   4. Projection (Psychology).   I. van Beusekom, Janneke.   II. Gibbons, Dorothy.   III. Title.

Cover design by Diana Puppin.

Contents

PART II: WAYS OF HANDLING PROJECTIONS

Preface

This book pertains to the mundane and to guidelines for acting in the everyday. While spokespersons for modern day society seem preoccupied with the dramatic and the heroic, the loud and attention-getting, the sensational and horrific, life for most of us is more ordinary. Yet it is in the small and frequently repeated exchanges that the ground is prepared for dealing with the large and most challenging ones. The meaning of life is in the living, in how we manage what attracts us in the world, in how we handle the emotionally lively interactions that arise in the course of the day. Democracy, as well, the highest expression of communal existence, depends importantly on how we discharge our social and political responsibilities every day, in conversation, in work life, in decisions at the dinner table and in our recreational groups, at church and on the ball field. We live in the here and now, not only "out and about" but also locally, with cousins and acquaintances, our parents and our classmates.

Believing this, we were led to look at how some emotionally fraught and socially provocative expressions—specifically racism, sexism, homophobia, anti-Semitism, classism, and other forms of hatred of outgroups or different others—crop up in daily living. We began by examining our own reactions to such experiences and by talking to others about their reactions when someone expresses a provocative statement such as a homophobic remark or an ethnic joke in their presence. Many of the people we talked to reported that they, too, are in a quandary when they hear such remarks. They disapprove of these remarks and feel uncomfortable, yet they also feel dissatisfied with the various responses they have tried. Their interest in this topic and their sometimes intense emotional reactions to our question encouraged us to pursue this familiar, almost incidental territory. This led us to solicit stories about people's experience with prejudice, not only what had been said to them but also how they had reacted in the face of these remarks.

What was most impressive to us was how unfinished the encounters were for those who told us their stories. They were still reverberating to the episodes, still angry, puzzled, frustrated, or defeated. We were touching on unhealed wounds in our seemingly innocent question. Their descriptions were profound and affecting. We had no trouble engaging in further discussion with folks who told us their stories, and as we did, even more stories were forthcoming. Tales multiplied.

But only to describe what takes place is limited because it makes of us and of those to whom we speak passive observers of the social scene. Diagnosis is much easier than treatment; hearing of difficult encounters is much simpler than thinking through what to do. With the pervasiveness of television, motion pictures, the radio, and other forms of immediate mass contact, we have too much become a nation of spectators. In doing so we have fostered our own powerlessness, even while we admire, even dote on, the actors, athletes, and politicians who focus on power, on being strong, aggressive, dominant, and invulnerable. Merely to obtain a hearing in society these days means that one must shout, or be offbeat, or say outrageous and untrue things. We are going against the grain, then, when we wish to draw attention to the ordinary as a source of life-affirming and power-enhancing activities. But that is what we are about in this book, and we promise those who follow us with an open mind that they will find opportunities to reflect on their own lives and to learn possibilities for making life more active and vital.

Understanding a complex and challenging situation without also knowing what might be done in the face of such a situation is limiting. Therefore, we have committed ourselves to push beyond understanding into a proposal of guidelines. Because life is creative, actions unfold in surprising ways and other people are part of what happens in such unfoldings; consequently, we cannot give specific steps for the doing of important acts. Your grandmother differs from ours, the timbre of your voice differs from ours, the music of your relationships may be more or less melodious than ours. These variations mean that we cannot prescribe solutions in any detailed way. Social scientists who want to control and predict the behavior of their subjects have it wrong. The creativity of each moment is what makes us human and makes us agents of our lives. That is a fortunate reality, we believe, because it leaves to each individual the responsibility and opportunity for finding her or his own way to make community. The creativity and unpredictability of the events in our lives are wellsprings for exciting, democratic communities.

Yet there are principles that can be decoded from examples of lively encounters that lead to differing results, principles that can serve to inform us of approaches that we might otherwise not have considered. And there are lessons, too, that show us the limitations of actions that we have thought to be just right. In a world that knows bigotry only too well, in which religions are too often built on hatred of others, in which allegiances with one's own group are narrow and focused on protection against feared others, in which discrimination in the negative sense of prejudice and dislike is commonplace—in such a world every endeavor that promotes reconciliation and connection ought to be welcomed. That is what we focus on in this book.

While we have used technical ideas and language drawn from psychology, we have worked to make our line of thought clear to any open-minded, intelligent person. We have no doubt that the subject matter is vital and will likely become even more so in the difficult future that seems indicated from the problems of today. How to meet others who challenge us emotionally, who differ profoundly from us, yet who are important in our ongoing lives, is a significant problem. We hope to contribute to making it a problem that inspires people to action.

We start from the perspective that whatever else they may entail, racist, sexist, homophobic, anti-Semitic, anti-Catholic, anti-Irish, etc. remarks are importantly projections. By projection we mean a particular form of perceiving oneself and others in one's world. In a projection, something of an emotionally rich quality that is coming into awareness is anxiety producing for the individual. As a consequence, in order not to become aware of that quality and also of the anxiety that will accompany such an awareness, the person attributes to another person some characteristic of comparable emotional force. Thus, if a person feels strong love (or fear, or dislike) toward someone in his or her vicinity and perceives that the feeling would create anxiety, the individual might instead become aware, in condemnatory fashion, of the immorality of a distant figure. The projection enables the person to perceive emotional intensity without owning (attributing to self) the particular feeling that had been stimulated. Jokes and ethnocentric remarks, along with sexist comments, are convenient and common vehicles of projections. Recognizing this—and it has been said many times in the past and is almost commonplace by now—we believe that what is clinical wisdom can be turned to good advantage in our broader social lives. Clinicians have considerable experience coming to terms with persons projecting upon them and upon others in the world, and that experience can be adapted to social living. This book is one attempt at such an adaptation.

When we adapt the insights of clinicians concerning the management of projections, we do not mean to make therapists of ordinary people. Rather, we intend to make available to ordinary people some new ways of dealing with something that is common in their lives. We will argue that persons are doing something already, and our intention is to appraise critically what is being done and to offer help in doing things more effectively. We do not expect perfection or even major advances as persons use these insights. Few therapists do well in everyday life when confronted with racist or sexist remarks, as we will illustrate. What we hope is that individuals will feel encouraged to try novel methods when involved in these matters and will feel the excitement that is possible as a result.

While we concentrate upon the mechanism called projection, we do not intend to "pathologize" persons who are being racist, sexist, homophobic, and so on. That is to say, while we believe that the projections involved in these actions are faulty projections and that the persons who are projecting can profit from an exchange that corrects the errors these involve, we do not construe the persons according to any psychopathological diagnosis. We believe that all persons project much of the time in daily discourse and that that does not qualify them (or us) as being psychopathological. Of course, given our personal histories and the disordered society in which we live, each of us has psychological problems, but these vary considerably among us, and the focus of our work is not on a given pathology behind racist expressions. All such expressions represent what is called in Gestalt therapy "creative adjustments," adjustments that served a positive purpose at one time and now serve less well than they did originally. Those who would pathologize these projections seem to substitute a psychological diagnosis for moral condemnation, and we are interested neither in diagnosing nor in condemning. We do oppose racism, sexism, homophobia, anti-Semitism, and other forms of discriminatory projections, but we wish to do so in a way that is respectful and egalitarian—not an easy task.

This book is not a scientific report nor is it a clinical case study. We have devoted ourselves to extended study of a common event, to thinking about this matter over a long period of time, to talking with friends and colleagues about what we have been finding, and to a simple play with ideas. We started to write a short article on projection in everyday life to follow up on our analysis of projection among professionals who work with victims (Gibbons et al. 1994). As we collected examples, raised our ideas and criticisms of how we and others managed to face projections at parties and in our homes, our ideas took on complexity and color. What was to be a short article evolved first into a longer one, then into a monograph, and finally into this book-length essay. We were taken over by our argument and by the reactions and challenges to our line of thought.

We have built this book around the formulation of a problem, using theory derived from common psychoanalytic and Gestalt therapy understandings, as well as many examples that we have collected. We do not pretend to have gathered examples from any "representative sample" that might give a ring of scientific generalizability to our work. Yet we have collected material from a variety of people in several differing contexts. The similarity and recognizability of the issues contained in these examples have convinced us that our analysis has broad relevance. We rely a great deal on resonance within the reader with respect to our examples. If the reader is open-minded and yet does not find familiarity in these examples, we will be much surprised. And open to correction.

Acknowledgments

Many people have contributed to this work and we can express our appreciation to only a small portion of them. We have had guidance and commentary from many sources, at parties, at conventions, at seminars and presentations, in daily discourse as well. Our work is truly a communal work, supported enthusiastically with suggestions, examples, challenges, and ongoing interest. We have leaned not only on scholars, whom we acknowledge in our bibliography, but students and friends, colleagues and acquaintances. To them all we are deeply indebted.

The following people have taken the additional step of detailing for us, either in written form or in extended discussion, examples from their experience. We owe them greatly and are happy to extend our appreciation. They are Raymond Albert, Jim Baumohl, Laura Cohen, Carol Finnegan, Olivia May Frazier, Yael Goldstein, Melanie Grossman, Patrice Heller, Valerie Huff, Celeste Johnson, Eileen Kenna, Sonja Lindgren, Jayne Oasin, Michael Pfeiffer, Inger Sandanger, Karen Smith, and Carol Swanson.

We have been supported throughout also by the Mary Hale Chase Fund at Bryn Mawr College. Our gratitude to Bryn Mawr goes far beyond the contributions from the fund.

And we are grateful indeed to those family members and friends who have supported us personally. Elsa R. Lichtenberg provided continuing personal nourishment as well as many books in the field of study, and I (P.L.) want to record my profound appreciation for all that she has given to me. I (J.v.B) am grateful to my husband, Alan Caniglia, for his invaluable support and to my children, Annelies and Ellie, for tolerating the innumerable Tuesdays when Mom was in Bryn Mawr meeting with her colleagues and working on their book. And I (D.G.) would like to thank my friends who treated me like family and my family who treated me like a friend throughout this project.

PART I

ON MUNDANE PROJECTIONS

A Common Occurrence

It happens all the time. Family and friends are gathered together for a celebratory feast, Thanksgiving, Easter, or a summer's picnic in the park. Conversation is bubbly and warm, or correct and measured, or relaxed and congenial, whatever way is usual for the set of family and friends who have come together. Then, usually quite unexpectedly, someone tells a racist or ethnic joke, or comments in a sexist way. The comment isn't limited to majority groups of society and could come from anyone: father, grandmother, uncle, brother-in-law, cousin, family friend, someone known for such an orientation by some or all of those present. And the comment makes a pronounced impact on the group. Maybe all laugh and appear to join in the fun, but there is usually an accompanying undercurrent of tension that no one wants to address. Maybe there is a favorite target in the circle—the daughter, perhaps, who is known for her feminist ways, the friend who has interracial ties, the too-liberal uncle who is outspoken in his concern for the impoverished, or the family member most reactive to the latest insulting experience he or she has had to endure for being gay or dark-skinned. Whatever the particular conjunction of persons, this scene is enacted in many different gatherings and rarely, if at all, is there a simple, happy resolution of the tensions raised in these gatherings. A certain unease prevails. But for the sake of peace or harmony or family unity no one responds directly to the rift that has been created in the group. Instead, people laugh politely or with exaggerated hilarity, or avert their eyes and change the subject, or withdraw emotionally from the scene. The attempted unity of feeling, if it *is* achieved, costs dearly, and much of the time withdrawal and divisiveness are the unhappy outcome. Individuals—including the one who has made the comment—leave these gatherings feeling tense or angry or upset, often unaware of what has occurred and puzzled by why they so frequently leave these family gatherings feeling disconcerted and disappointed.

These sexist or racist jokes and comments have such an adverse effect on a group because they are more than just inappropriate, impolite expressions. They are powerful projections that result from the projecting person's inability or unwillingness to handle strong feelings. These projections, which may temporarily relieve the person of intense, possibly painful, feelings, stir up unresolved conflicts in those people present so that the listeners become more than just uninvolved bystanders. The listeners, too, suddenly experience burdensome feelings and find themselves thrust into an emotionally charged situation in which they may have strong convictions about both the social views expressed in the projection and the person who has just projected. But because these projections have been injected into an apparently harmonious gathering, the pressure to collaborate is subtle—it appears not as a command but as an invitation. We use the terms *invitation* and *invitee* to emphasize the point that the listener cannot remain a complete observer to what is taking place. An invitation is a call to participate in something, whether it is an invitation to a wedding or an invitation to laugh at a joke. The listener is forced to respond in some way. Even a non-response is experienced by the person who has issued the invitation as a kind of statement. Accordingly, once an invitation is launched, a listener becomes an invitee, a willing or unwilling participant in a relationship.

As we discussed the various ways that people have responded to invitations to collaborate with projections, we became aware that among those people who refused to collaborate—regardless of how they chose to refuse—there was a strong sense of responsibility to address discriminatory remarks as well as strong desires to avoid turning against those family members and friends who made the remarks and to avoid causing turmoil in a social gathering. This book is an attempt to join with those who are grappling with ways to respond in sensible and responsible fashion, with those who choose to use these invitations as ways of encountering their own strong reactions to projections. Once a person has been invited to collaborate, he or she can no longer claim innocence or non-involvement. One can choose how to act in response to the invitation, but one's actions have an impact on oneself, on the projecting person, on the immediate surroundings, and on the larger social world.

We believe that the innumerable inhumane acts the world has witnessed—wars, genocide, centuries of oppression, and racially or religiously motivated crimes—are importantly a direct result of projections. And we further suspect that such horrifying acts have their roots in the unhealthy social relations that we create or allow to exist in those groups with which we interact on a daily basis: in our families, among our friends and acquaintances, and in our workplaces. The racist or ethnic jokes or the sexist comments casually shared "among friends" in these settings are more than just harmless expressions. They are important small-scale projections and they provide the soil from which emerge the more devastating projections entailed in large-scale animosities and oppression.

It is not exceedingly difficult to observe and diagnose projections, and such practices have become commonplace both in clinical settings and in everyday interactions. We have learned, however, by our experience and by a search of the professional literature that it is much easier to recognize and to label such processes than it is to do something productive when relating to a person who is actively projecting. Labeling allows us to remain objective and somewhat detached from the person projecting; this detachment protects us from becoming actively engaged with this person who is in the midst of an intense emotional experience and it safeguards us from becoming overwhelmed by those intense feelings that have been aroused within ourselves or the projecting person as a result of the projections. Relating to someone who is actively projecting is both difficult and taxing. People do not project onto others unless they feel bothered in some way by what they may come to experience and they may go to great lengths in social relations to avoid that inner awareness. Care must be taken when engaging in this enterprise lest the projecting person become overwhelmed by unmanageable feelings.

At the same time, not dealing with projections when they are in operation is costly to the participants and ultimately involves even more difficult problems. Misunderstandings, false conceptions, alienation, antagonism, and excessive self-control are all symptoms of unattended projecting processes. Faulty projections tend to cut off communication or to attenuate it and to lead to hostilities between individuals and also between groups.

The matter is further complicated by the fact that not all projections are faulty. In order that we might understand others, we must engage in empathy, a form of projection, and accordingly projection has a healthy basis and is necessary for human development as well as basic social relations. Matching similarities between self and other, in which nothing of self is lost, is healthy and fruitful projection, and we do not focus on those sorts of processes in this analysis. We are here concerned only with those projections that are faulty, those in which the individual loses part of the self by attributing something to a person or group outside of the self.

Furthermore, we are especially interested in those instances in which a person projects and invites another to collaborate. The projecting person who makes a sexist joke may expect members of his or her audience to join in the humor or to make a typical or expected objection to it so that a kind of teasing and taunting unfolds. The collaboration need not be congenial; it just needs to conform to an expected pattern. For example, if a man always gets a heated argument from his wife in response to his sexist remarks, then they have inadvertently created a way to collaborate around his projections. Repeated, familiar responses, whether they appear supportive or confrontational, may be somewhat comforting to the projecting person, even if not to his partner, but they will not enable the person to fully realize his or her purpose.

This book consists of two parts. In Part I we explore the following complex questions about the projection process:

What lies behind a person's compulsion to project?

How is the person who is projecting attempting to change his or her psychic reality through these projections?

How do such projections affect those who witness the projections and those who are invited to collaborate in these projections?

How do those who are present during the projection contribute—perhaps unwittingly—to the conditions that give rise to such projections?

How does the person who is projecting rely on the collaboration of others to complete the projection?

How do those who are invited to collaborate with projections in everyday situations facilitate or foster those projections— and the larger social consequences of such projections— by their unwillingness or inability to manage these invitations in an effective way?

In Part II we turn from analysis of what projections are about and what they bring up in those around the projecting person to a more proactive concern: What is one to do in such situations? We explore the differences between good handling and poor handling of invitations to collaborate with projections. We see good handling as responses that lead to the reowning of projections and to increased friendliness, while we see poor handling as responses that lead to more deeply entrenched projections and isolation. We are aware that there is no one correct response to projections and that people are often only partly effective when attempting to handle an invitation to collaborate. In this book we identify five common responses that constitute poor handling and discuss in detail how these responses are hurtful to both the projecting person and the invitee. We discuss how self-hatred is a basic issue underlying these projections. We propose that for good handling to ensue, the invitee must respond to the projecting person empathically while managing a complex inner experience. Needless to say, this last statement requires a good deal of elaboration, and a significant portion of Part II is devoted to fleshing out what we mean by good handling. Throughout this essay examples are used extensively to explain and support our theoretical work. We conclude with a chapter elaborating on some issues raised by this work and reflecting on their implications for human and social endeavors.

2

Principles of Faulty Projections

To be able to engage productively with a person who is actively projecting and who is inviting one to be a collaborator with that projection, a person must have some grasp of the basic principles of faulty projection. We believe that four such principles are especially helpful to our understanding of the process of projection and thus to our understanding of the projecting person. First, projection is partly a social phenomenon, for example, when it takes place in real or imagined social circumstances. The social situation that promotes projection is one in which the person who is projecting is experiencing too much arousal, given the support that is available for the handling of that aroused condition. We call this the arousal/support balance. Second, a projection enables a person to avoid awareness of possessing certain characteristics. By placing internal qualities outside of one's self, the projecting person avoids awareness of owning those thoughts, feelings, or desires that have been aroused and that would be experienced as burdensome if they were given full play in that person's awareness. The person is in fact aware of these thoughts, feelings, and desires, but he or she experiences them as belonging outside himself or herself. Thus, projection involves a special sort of awareness. Third, a projection helps the person to establish a sense of distance between the self and the disowned parts. The person is defining himself or herself by contrast with an other who carries the disowned elements of self. Fourth, a projection creates a fusion between the projecting person and the other, even though the person's purpose in projecting is to deny any connection between the self and the object of the projection. An understanding of each of these four principles of faulty projection is important in helping someone remain engaged with the person who is projecting while avoiding compliance with that projection.

Social relationships are the ground from which projections arise. These relationships are central to the arousal of thoughts, feelings, and desires in the parties to the relationship. Sometimes the social situation is responsible for instigating the arousal, as when an attractive person is seductive, a boss is demanding, a group engages in a ritual that is emotionally rich, or an invader attacks one's domain. At other times the social circumstance is merely the occasion for the expression of an aroused state, as when an already angry motorist is inconvenienced by traffic, an excited child comes home from school to relate her day's activities to her parents, or an athlete is imagining the contest that will test his or her abilities. Thus, one aspect of social conditions that facilitate projections is that they somehow are challenges to an individual, challenges that provoke thoughts, feelings, or desires that may become difficult to manage in the person's aware experience, challenges that produce heightened arousal.

However, social relationships also serve as supports to individuals in the handling of their experience. High arousal becomes troublesome only when the individual is left to his or her own devices to manage what comes up. The arousal can be any kind of excitement—love, anger, fascination, fraternal feeling. If others are present who can stay in close contact with the person experiencing challenging thoughts, feelings, or desires and who can enable the mastery of these, then projection becomes unnecessary. What is important is the support—self-support and social support—that is present to enable the experiencing of the arousal. Put together, then, imbalance in the proportion of social arousal to social support is ground for projection when the support is not adequate to the demands of arousal.

The avoidance of awareness of possessing certain thoughts, feelings, or desires, our second principle of faulty projection, comes into play when the needed support for the given arousal is not available. Laplanche and Pontalis (1973) further explain this second principle of projection: "The subject attributes tendencies, desires, etc., to others that he refuses to recognize in himself; the racist, for instance, projects his own faults and unacknowledged inclinations on to the group he reviles" (p. 351). Similarly, they state that projection "always appears as a defense, as the attribution to another (person or thing) of qualities, feelings or wishes that the subject repudiates or refuses to recognize in himself" (p. 352). In short, the person does not bear the burden of experiencing as part of himself or herself that which is seen as part of the external world. Many factors may contribute to this tendency: the feelings or thoughts are too bothersome to be owned, the person is accustomed to others carrying the emotional part of a relationship, or the individual may be psychologically lazy or incapable of tolerating certain subjective experiences. Regardless of the reasons a person has a tendency to project, the projection enables that person to split off and deny undesirable aspects of the self.

A projection not only rids the person of undesirable qualities; it also protects the projecting person from the reassimilation of those parts by creating a sense of distance between the person and the object of the projection. This is the third principle of projection. The projecting person places the unwanted feeling inside the other and negates that feeling by sharply differentiating self from the other: "He has that emotion; I do not." The projecting person then marshals defenses against an awareness that such a feeling may be his or her own by constantly focusing on and criticizing this alien quality within the other. By making external that which is internal, projections permit a person to deal with undesirable thoughts or desires at a greater distance—on a social rather than on an intrapersonal level. This distance creates an illusion of safety within the projecting person. However, to maintain this safe space, the projecting person must constantly guard against an invasion from the outside world of these split-off qualities, since the absence of these qualities is an important part of his or her self-definition.

Ironically, at the same time that the projecting person is distancing the other, or putting self over against the other, he or she is also becoming tied to or fused with that other. The feeling, thought, or desire has not disappeared and freed the person to act unencumbered; it has been split off and located in the object of the projection. As a consequence, the projecting person has become dependent on the other for the bearing of his or her experience. Without this other, the projecting person would have to experience the feeling, thought, or desire as his or her own, and one central function of projection is to avoid this eventuality. Thus, the projecting individual is intimately linked to the object of his or her projection. This dependency by way of fusion is the fourth principle of faulty projection.

It is important to note that the differentiating and merging that we have described in the third and fourth principles of projection are different from what appears in wholesome human encounters. In wholesome encounters, individuals become aware of and assert their feelings, thoughts, or desires openly and directly. Individuals do not split off the undesirable; rather, they stay with their experience and with the support of others they hold it, mold it, and integrate it into the self. This allows the engagement and appreciation of both similarities and differences among the parties involved. Consequently, they are not dependent on the other to be whole, and merging takes on a different texture. As a result of the negotiation of both the similarities and differences, the individuals together build a unified figure; they tend to merge into a "we" in which individuality, having been asserted, now becomes obscured. This is a productive playing out of the dialectic of self-assertion leading to fusion or confluence (Lichtenberg 1991).

Unlike the unhealthy fusion that results from faulty projection (with its accompanying diminishment of what is owned by the self), healthy fusion is experienced as highly rewarding by the participants and it facilitates personal growth. In wholesome human encounters, the autonomy or agency of the participants is enhanced and vivid before fusion, and the merging represents an expansion and enrichment of each individual through the creation of a unit larger than the self. After such a merging, each participant can withdraw and can assimilate into the self what has been experienced through a deep connection with another. All growth of the human personality relies on this interplay of autonomy and merging or "homonomy" (Angyal 1965), the trend toward becoming a part of a unit larger than oneself.

In unwholesome encounters with projection in force, any merging is a function of similarities among the participants; differences are allotted to "them," to outsiders who are the objects of projection. The self-assertion/fusion dialectic is distorted. Persons become confluent with one another not by announcing and resolving their differences with each other, but by putting differences in the outgroup formed by projection. The encounters tend to be deadly because neither the liveliness of difference nor the closeness of confluence is fully exploited. Thus, under projections, persons may "meet" their allies but not in a differentiated way, and they may be differentiated from outsiders whom they will not be able to "meet."

Because we believe that the self-assertion/fusion dialectic is so important in avoiding faulty projections and because we will later depend on the readers' understanding of this dialectic when we suggest guidelines for building satisfying, respectful relationships, we would like to examine this dialectic more closely. In doing so, we rely on the Gestalt therapy theory of the contact and withdrawal cycle (Perls et al. 1951), and on the special interpretation by the senior author (Lichtenberg 1987) of how this cycle describes wholesome human encounters.

According to the theory of Gestalt therapy, the contact and withdrawal cycle consists of four different stages: fore-contact, contact, final contact, and withdrawal or post-contact. These stages describe the ebb and flow of episodes in persons' lives.

In the fore-contact stage, an individual is discovering the various needs that are emerging from within as well as possibilities in various objects in the environment that can connect with such needs or arouse other needs, and that can be used as resources to build a satisfying figure through social interactions. In the contact stage, the person is actively identifying himself or herself with some of the needs from within and is actively selecting elements from the external world that can be integrated with these needs to create the satisfying figure. Also, in the Contact stage, the individual is putting aside those needs and demands that are not to be integrated into the gestalt or figure that is being formed in the action.

In these first two phases of the cycle, fore-contact and contact, the individual is involved in being an agent, in self-assertion or self-definition. Part of this self-assertion is promoting the other in his or her special otherness, his or her particularity, so that a fusion with the other will meet the needs of all parties to the encounter. Contact with an other means expressing one's special nature, and it also means facilitating the expression by the other of his or her special nature. In the final contact phase, there is a "meeting" or healthy confluence in which all parties merge. Each individual will lose self in the fusion that takes place. Finally, in the withdrawal stage, the persons withdraw from each other and assimilate what they have gained from the encounter. Importantly, the person's desire for and experience of the loss of self in final contact enhances the growth of the person. These wholesome meetings between persons provide the nourishment of human connection just as proper breathing and eating enable individuals to extract from the external world what is necessary for their existence and their growth.

From this healthy combination of self-assertion and merging arise both a distinct "I" and a distinct "you" (in the contact phase of the cycle) and a consequent "we" (in the final contact phase of the cycle). Unhealthy forms of the cycle involve a diminution of one or another of these characteristics. There may be a distinct "I" with a fuzzy "you" as in moments of domination in which the other is impeded in defining self. There may be a distinct "you" and a fuzzy "I" as in moments of sacrifice and submission. And there may be limitations or inhibitions upon "we-ness" in those encounters in which confluence is demanded prematurely, without the full unfolding of the involved participants, that is, in which the "we-ness" is a means to avoid awareness of a distinct "I" or "you" during the other phases of the cycle.

Each of the four principles of faulty projection encroaches on the dialectic of defining self and merging with an other. Instead of acknowledging and accepting various qualities within themselves and others, projecting persons rush to confluence. These faulty projections distort the person's experience in the contact and withdrawal cycle so that the person neither fully individuates nor fully merges.

In conclusion, the four basic principles underlying faulty projections can be summarized as follows:

1. Social situations that stimulate high arousal but do not provide adequate support for what is aroused in an individual may promote faulty projections.
2. Faulty projections place internal qualities outside the self, thereby allowing some experience of these qualities but at the cost of keeping the person unaware that these are qualities of the self.
3. Faulty projections create a sense of distance between the individual and the object of the projection.
4. Yet, as a result of faulty projections, the individual is tied to or fused with the object of the projection.

Invitations to Collaborate with Projections

When a person voices a faulty projection in the presence of another person, he or she has issued an invitation to collaborate with that projection. Invitations to collaborate share the basic principles of an unvoiced, faulty projection. In fact, we believe that the person issuing the invitation is attempting to enlist others in bolstering one or another aspect of these principles that the projecting person assumes is ineffective as long as the projection remains unvoiced. In other words, if a wish becomes strong enough that it threatens to enter a person's awareness, the person may not only project but may also solicit support of others in keeping this wish out of awareness.

Below is an example of an invitation to collaborate with a projection. In the analysis that follows the example, we examine how each principle of projection plays out in invitations to collaborate with projections.

"One of my younger sisters is dating an African-American man and my father is furious about this. He puts me in an awkward position because he makes disparaging remarks about my sister for dating the man, and I know he expects me to agree with him. My father knows I don't disapprove of my sister's interracial dating but he continues to make racist remarks in my presence and I don't know what to say. I can see that my father is upset and I feel sorry for him, but I don't want to turn my back on my sister. Most of the time I just keep quiet when my father gets started on this topic."

When Dad asks his eldest daughter to join him in condemning her sister for interracial dating, he is inviting her to collaborate with his racism. And he may do this even though he knows that his eldest daughter holds beliefs more like her sister's than like his. Something interesting is going on here, something significant in Dad's handling of feelings that pertain both to his eldest daughter and to her sister. The sister's choice of dating partner is one piece of the puzzle, and we can imagine that she may have brought up jealous and sexual feelings in Dad. After all, what is more common than a father's rivalry with his daughter's partner? And interracial dating often brings up sexual associations, especially in vividly prejudiced persons, as we know historically from segregationist movements. Alternatively, the feelings aroused in Dad might be anger at her disobedience or her independence, or shame that he would be seen as having a daughter who is dating someone from another race. Further, the father's relation to his eldest daughter is another piece of the puzzle. Wanting her to join his castigation of her sister may be Dad's way of managing his own arousal by creating a shared moral judgment, intensively held.

What we see in an invitation to collaborate with a projection, then, is an effort to handle the emotional condition that is present not only by the original method of projecting but also by shoring up that projection through mobilization of an ally. There is activated a kind of second-order projection, one that depends on social support for its continuance. Creation of a collaborator with the projection is a means for deeper dealing with the four principles that undergird projection in the first place: readjusting the proportion of social arousal to social support, avoiding awareness of what has been aroused, distancing from the object of projection, and fusing with an other. Let us see how this looks with respect to Dad and his daughter.

In the example related above, Dad's available support was not adequate to meet the challenge of the arousal he felt when he discovered his daughter was dating interracially. In addition, an unvoiced projection was not sufficient for him to manage all that had been raised in him. He attempted to garner the necessary support by inviting his eldest daughter to collaborate with the projection. Had she agreed with Dad, she would have provided him with some support so that there would have been more support relative to what had been aroused. Dad would have been relieved that he was not alone and overburdened with his emotions.

Daughter's agreement, however, would have kept Dad further from awareness of exactly what feelings had been aroused. If interracial dating makes Dad ashamed in his social circle, or he imagines that it will, daughter's agreement may confirm that shame. Meanwhile, Dad may become increasingly ignorant of what underlies the shame, what of the young woman's behavior threatens him specifically and directly. Is her independence frightening? Is he jealous? Is her disobedience a sign of his weakness, which he finds intolerable? What might at first seem self-evident in his arousal is probably complex, and the hidden desires have become more unavailable by the eldest daughter's support.

Furthermore, if Dad had received his eldest daughter's collaboration, he would have created an in-group consisting of himself and his eldest daughter, while placing her sister in the out-group; it would now be father–eldest daughter versus the offending daughter. The eldest daughter's collaboration would distance her father from her sister even more. By identifying members of the in-group, Dad would have made the out-group more distinct. By creating a haven of in-group members (Dad, sister, and possibly other family members as well), Dad would have symbolically created a fortress that would be strongly defended against invasion from what was split-off and called foreign. Part of the eldest daughter's quandary would be her sense that, through her collaboration, she too would be alienating her sister.

Finally, Dad now would have two fusions to help him deal with what is uncomfortable. First, he would have the overt confluence from the collaboration of the eldest daughter; he would be fused with her and dependent on her to maintain the in-group in which all acceptable feelings and motivations are ensconced. And second, he would have the covert fusion with his other daughter who is dating in defiance of his will; he would depend on her to be the repository of what he cannot own and accept in himself. Now Dad's need to fuse is more amply accommodated.

Of course, the eldest daughter, caught between Dad and her sister, may choose not to join with Dad. She may decide to ally herself with her sister or try to stay in the background. If she were successful in allying herself with her sister, or if her father would not allow her to recede into the background, what would happen is quite predictable. Eldest daughter would become proxy for her sister and be put in the out-group by Dad. Now it would be Dad versus his two daughters, and the intensity of Dad's projections would increase. He would have changed the arousal/support balance in an unfavorable direction, would have had his unawareness threatened, would have distanced both daughters, and would have only his unaware fusion at his disposal. His attempt to shore up his projection would have failed and he would be in a worse predicament than before.

Such invitations to collaborate with projections are common among most racial groups. For example, projecting upon whites is a common device used to express in-group solidarity among African-Americans, and the consequences of these projections are commonly underestimated. The demands for loyalty are intense, and contempt for those who seem not to be completely joined with the in-group (those called "Uncle Tom" or "Aunt Jemima" or "oreo") is frequently voiced. But we believe that projections upon whites—the underpinning of "cultural paranoia"—carry the same costs as projections upon other out-groups by any in-group. In the following example, our narrator (an African-American woman in an in-group of African Americans) was put off by two friends.

"Several of my friends were sitting around the table and discussing events and news items. One of them was my lover who I knew disliked white people. He had told me that when we got married (which we never did), I would give up my white friends. I told him not to ever bring up the subject again. As usually happens, the subject of white people came up. Someone said that no white person was ever to be trusted. My friend, Mary, said a white man would sell his mother if he got the chance. I excused myself and went to the kitchen to wash the dishes. I have never forgotten the way she said that."

The narrator showed no sign of knowing what is going on around the table at the moment that precipitated the projections; yet she intuitively knew that she did not want to collaborate and the incident had a long-term effect on her.

These projections, which create sharp divisions along racial lines, pose special problems for biracial individuals. Lise Funderburg (1994) interviewed forty-six persons who were identified as biracial; they had one black parent and one white. Here are two examples taken from her study.

"The African-American community at Penn is pretty militant, and they don't want you to hang out with white people. There was a W.E.B. Du Bois house where you lived if you were a 'progressive' African-American. I could never find out when black student union meetings were because I lived in High Rise North and they didn't want to put signs there because they were afraid that white people were going to come. I know because I asked the guy who was president of the African-American student union, and he said, 'We can't get anything done with those people crashing the meeting. You know how those people are.'

"I feel like I can never be a very militant African-American person who hates white people because I'd hate fifty percent of myself. I think the black students just wrote me off. . . . And maybe I'm making this up, but I think they saw me a lot of times with white people and I got blacklisted." [p. 136]

"Now I know I can relax with you," said one black woman when she discovered that a white-looking acquaintance was biracial. "I know that you're not going to say something ignorant all of a sudden."

Once a racial allegiance is established, the biracial person is assumed to be part of one group, and so, by definition, not part of any other. People who would never criticize another racial group directly will often let slip a prejudice if they think they are surrounded by their own. These gems can shine at any moment, in any conversation. Waiting for that comment, that disappointment, hangs menacingly over new relationships. As a number of biracial people said, "I am always waiting for the other shoe to drop." [p. 154]

The dynamics involved in these examples are typical of many invitations to collaborate with a projection. If the projecting person finds a way to assimilate and take back what was disowned, his or her need to invite others to participate might not arise. However, when this does not happen, the projecting person is compelled to look outside and to invite one or more others to collaborate with his or her projection. Unfortunately, though, such invitations to collaborate often decrease the person's chances of attaining adequate help in reowning what has been projected. Invitations focus attention on the content of the projection rather than on the person's motivation to project; by asking others to focus "out there" on the external world, the person is diverting attention away from himself or herself and the aroused state that prompted the projection. Consequently, if others do collaborate with the projection, the person is receiving support to keep external something he or she has already disowned and this support actually prevents the person from effectively managing the heightened feelings that led to the projection.

The projection process is replete with these kinds of contradictions, and invitations to collaborate take participants through a field of inconsistencies and convoluted messages, confusing all involved and limiting the ability of others to meet the aroused needs of the projecting person. What has been aroused within the projecting person is often very different from what he or she conveys to others. Therefore, while seeking to bolster the projection, the projecting person often diminishes his or her chances of attaining adequate support to help manage the aroused feeling. Let us explore further some of the contradictions in this process and illustrate how these contradictions derive from the issues underlying the four principles of faulty projecting.

In a heightened state of anxiety, the person who projects often dichotomizes the world and believes that "you are either with me or against me" when demanding support. To be "with me," the invitees are expected to accept unconditionally the projecting person's statements. To receive this unconditional acceptance, the projecting person often turns to those people with whom he or she feels the closest bond and asks for total agreement despite the fact that on other occasions these invitees may have clearly indicated that they do not hold the social views expressed in the projection. For example, even though Dad knows that his daughter does not hold similar views toward African-Americans, he hopes that the importance of the relationship between himself and his daughter will outweigh her commitment to differing social views and that she will be swayed to collaborate through a sense of loyalty. Surely, Dad hopes, the father–daughter bond preempts any allegiance to a political ideal and is stronger than any sibling bond. Although the bond between them may be strong enough to transcend political differences, Dad is not asking his daughter to provide him with emotional support despite their different social views. He is demanding complete agreement with the content of his projection, an agreement that to him symbolizes that emotional support. However, by being indirect and sending his daughter a convoluted message (i.e., "agree with me" rather than "support me in this difficult time"), Dad in fact impairs his ability to muster the social support he so desires. We also see this insistence on loyalty quite clearly when the African-American woman's lover suggests that marriage means she must dismiss her white friends—which she had no intention of doing.

Persons issuing invitations to collaborate may also diminish their chances for attaining social support by creating misleading images of themselves as they proffer these invitations. For example, projections are often made forcefully and confidently, as if the person is coming from a position of strength; yet the reality is that the person is feeling somehow threatened, weak, and in need of external support. However, given the illusion of strength that the projecting person creates, there is little likelihood that the person invited to collaborate will fully recognize the projecting person's need for that support. Also, because one of the principal functions of projection is to enable the person to deny the existence or meaning of the intensely aroused emotion, the projecting person often couches the projection in the form of a joke or a casual, offhand remark, thereby deflecting attention away from this need for help. In this way, a serious matter is trivialized. When invitees respond to the apparent frivolity and insignificance of a remark in likewise fashion, the likelihood is very high that the projecting person will receive less than the desired degree of support.

In addition, the projecting person often decreases his or her opportunity to receive emotional support by explicitly focusing on an intellectual abstraction or political opinion and by soliciting agreement with his or her argument. At best, he or she can expect confirmation for the expressed opinion but this confirmation is a far cry from meeting the personal and emotional needs that are at stake in the midst of the person's arousal/support crisis.

Aside from seeking to increase support for what has been aroused, the person who issues the invitation to collaborate also seeks help in allocating troublesome feelings to the external world. These feelings do not feel safe or manageable to the projecting person, and so he or she tries to alienate the feelings by placing them outside. Ironically, though, those who collaborate also validate the projecting person's fears. The result is that the projecting person's sense of danger is increased now that others agree that these attributes are "out there" where they are less easily controlled. Objects of projection are now perceived as antagonists, ready to launch an attack. Thus, instead of creating a safer world, the projecting person has found people to cooperate in creating an image of a more dangerous world.

The feelings that are allocated to the external world are not always troublesome feelings. Sometimes the projecting person seeks help in keeping good feelings rather than hostile or negative feelings external. Persons who have been taught to suppress an awareness of all feelings, including feelings of closeness, love, or sexuality, may be overwhelmed by the arousal of such good feelings in unusually intimate moments or at happy gatherings of family or friends. If they have adopted the belief that the awareness and expression of such feelings is unacceptable, they may project their feelings onto an out-group as a means of lessening the internal tension. Because an awareness of these feelings is unacceptable to the projecting person, the feelings are often projected onto others as unredeeming qualities; for example, an enjoyment of warm feelings may be projected as moral lassitude, or healthy sexuality may be projected as promiscuity. If the projecting person is successful in enlisting others to bolster the projection, that is, to attribute the feelings to others rather than to himself or herself, then the person has actually solicited assistance in reinforcing the sense that feelings, even positive ones, are dangerous to possess and need to be guarded against.

Aside from seeking help in creating distance and safety from unmanageable aspects of a situation, the projecting person often seeks the warmth and closeness of fusion with the collaborators. The voiced projection, however, may be one of anger and hatred at those relegated to the out-group. By channeling all negative feelings elsewhere, the projecting person hopes to bring members of the in-group closer to one another while presenting himself or herself as one who radiates warmth and good feelings. However, the hostility underlying the projection belies the benevolent image the projecting person attempts to create, and potential collaborators may distance rather than connect with the person because they are confronted with an atmosphere of antagonism rather than one of warmth and closeness.

Because the projecting person seeks ine support, even fusion, with the others present, he or she will often attempt to minimize the risk of losing social support when inviting others to collaborate. The person will project onto a group that does not appear to have the allegiance of those who are present, as when a man working out with his male friends at a gym makes a sexist remark concerning women or gay people. Believing that this is not the time to provoke controversy and risk losing social affiliation, the individual is likely to target groups that he or she somehow believes are already less than acceptable to those in his or her audience. Interestingly, while the individual acts as if he or she is part of the in-group by voicing the projection in a group that he or she expects will be supportive, the projecting person also doubts his or her full membership, as is evidenced by the need to pressure—or even to demand—that those present agree and thereby prove that they constitute a tightly knit in-group. This underlying distrust, in the presence of apparent trust, again fosters distance rather than the fusion intended by the projecting person.

The various contradictions inherent in invitations to collaborate that hinder a person's attempt to manage his or her internal life are not mutually exclusive; often many of these contradictions are in operation at once, creating an impasse and confounding the situation for all involved. The person who initiated the projection is disconcerted and does not know why, despite much effort to shore up the projection, he or she does not feel adequately met. The invitee, who is usually unaware of all that has motivated the person to project, becomes confused and immobilized because of the contradictions contained in these invitations to collaborate.

To summarize, when an individual makes a racist, sexist, or homophobic remark at a social gathering, that person is trying to correct an imbalanced arousal/support condition by mobilizing others to collaborate with the projection he or she is manifesting. Issuing an invitation to collaborate with the projection reveals in a social context the four principles of faulty projecting. However, the push toward support for the person's projection creates contradictions that limit the effectiveness of the projecting person's effort to solve an inner problem by socially distancing from an out-group and by demanding confluence through that distancing endeavor.

In the next chapter we turn our attention more fully to the effects on the invitee of being the recipient of these invitations.

4

What Comes Up in the Invitee?

When a projecting person invites another to collaborate with the projection, the other tends to be drawn into the present process and is significantly affected. Those who are affected by the invitation to collaborate we call "invitees," and we consider them to be an integral part of the projecting process.

We believe that the issues underlying projection can be as important to the invitee as they are to the person who is projecting. When presented with an invitation to collaborate with a projection, the invitee may find himself or herself in a vulnerable state similar to the arousal/support crisis that originally prompted the other person to project. Intense feelings similar to those that were affecting the projecting person may be brought up in the invitee. If the invitee does not feel that sufficient support is available to help contain the increased internal tension, the invitee will feel threatened and, therefore, may feel compelled to engage in a projection process of his or her own in an attempt to manage these newly aroused feelings. In other words, the invitee who feels vulnerable will often parallel the behavior of the person who initially projected.

The invitee may become involved in this parallel process either by *joining* the person around the original projection or by *distancing* from that individual. For instance, if a friend complains about all teenagers being heavily into drugs and sex and the invitee rapidly agrees without thoughtful consideration of the validity of this generalization, the invitee has joined the person around his or her projection and is likely to experience some emotional arousal. If, conversely, the invitee ridicules the person for asserting such a foolish idea, he or she has distanced from that individual. In either case, the invitee who does not have adequate support for the new level of arousal tends to mirror the defensive processes of the projecting person, to maintain the schema of in-group/out-group, and to prevent both participants in the encounter from reaching an awareness of the feelings that have led to their projections.

Although an invitee who joins appears to react very differently from one who distances, both experience a similar process before choosing to join or distance. Both experience arousal in response to the invitation to collaborate, both feel unsupported in acknowledging and containing such feelings, both avoid ownership of these feelings, and both project these feelings onto an external object. They differ in that the invitee who joins places the undesirable feelings onto the out-group that was targeted in the original projection, for instance, in this case the teenagers, while the invitee who distances places the undesirable feelings onto the person who initiated the projection, the friend who complained about teenagers. Yet just before the decision is reached about whether to join or distance, invitees are having common experiences.

Regardless of who becomes the object of the invitee's projection, teenager or friend in our example here, the invitee has created distance between the self and that object. Yet the invitee has also unknowingly become fused with that object because the invitee now uses that object of the projection to carry his or her split-off feelings. Therefore, although they emphasize different aspects of the projection process, invitees who join and those who distance are similar in that they both experience new arousal of feelings and believe that they lack the necessary support to contain these feelings. Accordingly, neither can react in an empathic way to the person who invited them to collaborate. Rather than becoming aware of and accepting their own strong feelings, persons who join and persons who distance react defensively. Through this defensive re-action, they break contact with both themselves and the person who is projecting. They are therefore unable to provide themselves or the other with the type of supportive environment that makes it safe for people to reown uncomfortable feelings. Instead of encourag-ing a wholesome human encounter in which the invitee and the projecting person could meet around both similarities and differ-ences, the invitee tends to carry forward the other's agenda that one must declare an allegiance to an in-group or an out-group. This reinforcement of either/or thinking heightens the participants' sense of vulnerability in relation to their own strong emotional experiences as well as their sense of danger in relation to differences in the external world.

Despite these basic commonalities between joining and dis-tancing, the invitee's subjective experience of joining the project-ing person will be very different from his or her experience of dis-tancing from that individual. Invitees who on a given occasion join or collaborate with a projection are declaring an allegiance to the in-group and are joining efforts with the person initiating the pro-jection in keeping the undesirable qualities "out there" in a mutu-ally agreed-upon out-group. Frequently, such invitees have their own history of projecting onto the same out-group and they share the social views expressed in the projection. Telling a racist joke to an avowed racist is likely to bring an in-group laugh. As well-established members of the in-group, participants may take turns initiating and collaborating with projections so that any one projection is a spe-cific expression of a larger, ongoing projection, and among mem-bers of the in-group participation in these projections is a sign of affinity with the group. In such cases, an invitation to collaborate with a particular projection appears to be accepted automatically and seems to provide the invitees with a sense of relief and solidarity as they ally themselves with the person who is projecting and shore up their defenses against the agreed-upon threat of the out-group.

Since these projections are part of an ongoing alliance among the collaborators, there appears to be little or no risk for the person who offers the invitation to collaborate, no hesitation among those accepting the invitation, and "no harm done" by everyone sharing a laugh over a sexist joke or a homophobic remark. However, as a result of the collaboration, both the person initiating the projection and the invitees remain alienated from their internal discomfort. In addition, their sense of vulnerability against the particular out-group has been—at least temporarily—increased. Although collaboration may briefly relieve the invitees of the anxiety aroused in the presence of the invitation to project, collaboration also increases the sense of danger in the world. This sense of danger will eventually lead to further anxiety and projections and a more deeply entrenched belief that one is quite vulnerable in a hostile world. This belief then reinforces the cycle of anxiety, projection, and fear.

Frequently, the social support that both the projecting person and the invitees receive in such collaborations is based on the assumption that the participants are already joined because they share some similar characteristics: they are all males, or all African Americans, or all members of the same family. Often this immersion within a particular group may be so integral to a person's identity that the person has not differentiated enough from the in-group to question that group's assumptions and projections. However, feelings are experienced individually, and the invitee who feels anxious or vulnerable or fearful in the presence of a projection and who does not have a developed-enough sense of self to contain these feelings becomes more anxious and aroused as he or she experiences feelings that are not acknowledged by other members of the in-group. The invitee then seeks to burrow deeper into this alliance with the in-group because disagreement with the in-group—or even having feelings that are different from those espoused by other members—arouses the possibility of being rejected and exiled from the haven of the in-group. For such persons, a sense of self is usually felt as something potentially dangerous, possibly leading to a lack of social support or ostracism, and so such persons may continue to seek and depend on a fusion with the in-group rather than risk annihilation in an attempt to discover a personal identity by differentiating self from other members of the in-group.

Without being grounded as a separate self, though, the invitee cannot support difference and, therefore, needs to reinforce the projection process that keeps heterogeneity among in-group members out of awareness. In this way, the invitee who collaborates with the projecting person with the intention of creating distance between the self and the out-group actually creates a covert fusion with the out-group that now serves to contain all differences for the invitee. And the sense of closeness that the invitee intended to create with the projecting person is now obscured because neither the invitee nor the person projecting has enough self-definition to make satisfying contact with the other.

Those invitees who choose to distance rather than join in reaction to an invitation to collaborate with a projection do so by exaggerating the differences between themselves and the person inviting them to collaborate. Such invitees tend to denigrate the person who initiated the projection and to reassure themselves that only unenlightened people experience racist, homophobic, or religiously biased feelings. They believe at such moments that they are in no way racist, sexist, and so forth. However, by exaggerating the differences, these invitees are paradoxically creating their own projections, this time placing the projecting person in an out-group of the unenlightened while declaring themselves to be members of an ideal in-group that only experiences feelings of love and acceptance toward others. Sometimes this distancing is characterized by angry attacks on the person who originally projected, with the invitee accusing the other of being a bigot, a racist, or a narrow-minded fool. At other times this distancing is characterized by silence and inner condemnation of the other.

Through this counterprojection process, these invitees manage to keep their own complex feelings in unawareness. For example, in the presence of a projection, an invitee may suddenly experience a quickening of his or her own racist, sexist, or homophobic attitudes, attitudes that may contradict the invitee's conscious social views and that the invitee wants to disown. By isolating these feelings as the characteristics *only* of the person who initially projected, the invitee manages to deny having any feelings that would threaten his or her image of being liberal and open-minded. Yet this form of projection also intimately links the invitee to the "narrow-minded" other because the invitee is now dependent on this other to be the bearer of his or her unacceptable thoughts and feelings.

Through distancing, invitees have also reinforced the belief that the world is dichotomized, although they have changed the in-group/out-group configuration so that the projecting individual who was attempting to rally in-group support is now denounced as a member of an out-group. And, ironically, while righteously attempting to separate themselves from the projecting person and to refuse the invitation to collaborate, these invitees inadvertently cooperate with the projection process: like the other, these invitees attempt to manage uncomfortable feelings through projection, thereby collaborating with the process though not with the specific content of the original projection.

In our discussion of distancing, we have interpreted that when a racist comment is made, the latent racism in persons who are invited to collaborate with a projection is stimulated and this stirring leads toward projections on the part of invitees. While we think this is most probably true since our society has been deeply racist, sexist, homophobic, classist, and so on, and this would mean we are all in some degree carriers of such orientations, we can also make a somewhat less strong statement. When a projecting person is seeking collaboration, he or she is demanding premature confluence.

The invitee's response may be more focused on resistance to such fusion than on having had his or her own animosities stimulated. That is, the demand for confluence may activate in the invitee some resentment or guilt (Polster and Polster 1973), and this reaction to the demand for confluence may then be primary rather than an internal response to one's own racism.

Similarly, the invitee may not be reacting to his or her own racism or to the demand for confluence, but simply to other introjects that have been touched. Thus, at a wedding one does not engage in intense interactions other than celebrating the couple. Here is a custom, a pattern of behaving that has been learned through the acquisition of manners. If one is "proper," one will follow this internalized command. Being proper may be more important to the invitee than being antiracist. However, this simpler explanation of the behavior of invitees seems to fail to account for the intensity of invitees' reactions and it also does not speak to how long these reactions remain unfinished business.

Accordingly, we can accept the idea that the reactions of invitees are more likely to refer to demands for confluence than to simple proprieties, although we continue to believe that underlying issues such as racism, sexism, homophobia, and classism, are being stimulated in these encounters.

Often an invitee will not know whether to join or distance and will attempt to avoid actively reacting to a projection by remaining silent, laughing politely, or in some way ignoring the invitation to collaborate. Such invitees are usually differentiated enough from the projecting person or from the in-group to have different beliefs and views but may not, at times, feel adequate support to verbalize this difference. In an attempt to protect themselves, to keep the peace, or to maintain a connection with the projecting person, these invitees may refrain from responding directly to the invitation, telling themselves that this is not a real collaboration since they are silently disagreeing with the content of the projection. However, by not openly asserting their truth and by not offering some counterpoint to the projecting process, these invitees are actually facilitating the process. Regardless of how the person offering the invitation interprets an invitee's noncommittal response, such an invitee has psychologically distanced from the projecting person and assumed no responsibility, in order perhaps to avoid conflict with the other. These broken contacts may allow both the invitee and the other to remain unaware of owning the feelings that have been aroused and may reinforce the belief that openly acknowledged differences threaten human relationships, a belief that fosters projections onto out-groups.

When these invitees do not respond openly to the invitation, they distance not only from the projecting person but also from others in the vicinity. We see this commonly at the family gatherings or parties when invitees imagine that if they express themselves strongly, they will violate the norms of congeniality on such occasions. The invitees project (often accurately, but sometimes falsely) that the hosts will be appalled at such open disagreement at a social event, and remaining silent they keep themselves hidden from others around them. The avoidance of open differences has become much more normative on social occasions in modern times than was once the case. In the past, roaring discussions of religion and politics were expected, and they often involved intense disagreement along with intense excitement and camaraderie. The lack of these experiences in our social circles is a fascinating contrast to the violence and mayhem that we see on television today.

When one is invited to collaborate with a projection involving in-group/out-group formations, that person is thrust into a new situation that is emotionally charged and that represents a challenge to the invitee. The tendency to engage in projections of one's own is fostered and following this tendency creates its own set of problems.

5

What Is Happening in the Transaction?

So far we have considered the experiences of the projecting person and the invitee separately and, for the sake of clarity, have isolated the invitation to collaborate with a projection from the transactional features of the relationship that exist between the projecting person and the invitee. These transactional characteristics always exist even if the participants have just met. Invitations to collaborate, like projections, always occur within the context of a social relationship; they evolve from and have an effect on those transactions. Yet so often the invitation confounds the relationship since it appears to come out of nowhere and to interrupt or dramatically change what has been happening between the participants. Several facets of these encounters stand out as important matters that may inform further our understanding of what is hoped for by the person who invites a collaboration with a projection and of what is experienced by the invitee of such a beckoning. In the examples we have collected, these facets seem to appear quite regularly.

First, within the transactions the participants are somehow becoming closer. Whether we are observing long-standing relationships, such as those between family members or among old friends, or new and even transient relationships, such as being introduced to a potential acquaintance or meeting someone at a bar and

engaging in friendly banter, the movement in the encounter is usually toward increased intimacy. This factor makes the issue of fusion
significant with respect to what is happening right now in the transaction. There is movement in the transaction toward confluence,
but the invitation to collaborate with the projection asks for too
much fusion too soon. The pacing of the contact and withdrawal
cycle is amiss.

Further, along with the closeness, there is usually an atmosphere of relative safety, an atmosphere that promises an in-group
alliance. The person who is projecting counts on good feeling and
safety in risking what he or she is doing. These elements of increasing intimacy and an increasing sense of safety are somehow associated with the experience of rising arousal in the participants. Heightened emotions may derive from the conditions of felt closeness and
safety or they may come from feelings of love, desire, hate, fear, or
discontent that have been otherwise stimulated. These feelings may
come from the social interaction itself, from the anticipations associated with the occasion, or from the loosening attendant upon
drinking alcohol. Whatever its source, the increasing arousal puts
a premium on both parties to support such excitement in the ongoing transaction.

In addition, the exact nature of the arousal in the projecting
person is obscure in the encounter, giving the scene a tone of mys-
tery to those involved. What has been stirred up in the person who
projects needs to be kept hidden, out of his or her awareness, so all
parties to the encounter are left to some degree in the dark about
what is going on. This leads to a final common component of such
transactions: the invitee is taken by surprise. The invitation to collaborate, whether directed toward a willing collaborator or one who
is offended, is tangential to what has been taking place up to that
moment. Something new or intrusive is injected into the encounter. A new demand is being introduced, and the invitee suddenly
feels challenged by the invitation to collaborate with the other's
projection.

Several examples may be helpful in illustrating the common ingredients of intimacy, safety, and surprise in transactions in which a person is invited to collaborate.

I had an awkward incident happen to me when I started a new job as a social worker at a drug and alcohol rehabilitation center. One of my co-workers on this new job happened to be a man I had worked with briefly on a former job. I didn't know him well, but since we were acquainted with one another, the director suggested that he show me around on my first day at work. As he described the center to me, he made it obvious that he was frustrated by some of the shortcomings of the program and that he blamed the director and other staff members for the program's lack of success. He listed many of their faults, including that many of them were recovering alcoholics or drug users themselves. He then said, "No wonder the program has so many problems, we have a bunch of addicts in charge."

I was stunned and offended by his comment, especially since I, too, am a recovering alcoholic. I wanted to tell him that I was insulted by his remark, but I didn't want to start an argument with someone on my first day at work. I also wondered if he had heard from others at our former workplace that I was a recovering alcoholic and if he was provoking me in some way. I felt the safest response was to make a general comment. I replied by saying, "Some of the most effective D and A counselors are people in recovery since they have had a personal experience with the struggle against addiction."

Even though I had spoken up in defense of recovering addicts, I left the conversation feeling dissatisfied and angry. For days afterward, I felt uncomfortable around this man because I felt as though he had tricked me into taking sides with him against the others. And I just did not feel good about not being honest about my own background even though I told myself that I had a right to keep my past private.

My friend had just moved into a neighborhood of old houses
and was talking to one of her new neighbors in the neighbor's
home. They got onto the subject of home renovation. The
woman who was host for this visit remarked that she had
painted her house two years earlier, and now she was bemoan-
ing the necessity of repainting. She pointed to paint already
peeling on a window sill and said, "What can you expect? They
took the lead out of all the paint because the niggers let their
children eat paint chips. Now the rest of us have to suffer. I
have three children, and I managed to keep them from eating paint." My friend was so startled and offended that she immediately got up, saying she had to leave. She did not confront
her neighbor or tell her why she was leaving, but left as quickly
as possible.

A group of Jewish women were conversing in a diner
that they had patronized for many years. The owner, who had
known them for many years, came over and in the course of
his conversation with them made a disparaging remark about
Jews and their money-grubbing ways. The women were astonished and hurt, but said nothing. After they left the diner, they
agreed that they would boycott the man's business. They felt
the remark had been especially hurtful since they had considered him to be a friend.

As is usual in most invitations to collaborate with a projection,
surprise was a central ingredient in each of these examples. The
invitees were "stunned," "startled," or "astonished" by the projecting person's attempt to create an in-group alliance by inviting them
to join forces against an out-group. In all these cases, the invitees
were offended, felt challenged by the invitation, and refused to
collaborate. Instead, they distanced themselves from the person who
was projecting. Although the distancing was more obvious with the
neighbor and the Jewish women, because they left the scene, the

social worker, too, created distance by psychologically withdrawing from the interaction. And in all three cases the invitees seemed unfinished and unsettled with the transaction.

Although the invitees were surprised by the invitations, there were facets of each relationship immediately preceding the invitation that may have forewarned the invitees of the possibility that an invitation was imminent. First, in each transaction there was the movement toward friendly closeness. Second, there was a growing atmosphere of safety. Finally, in each encounter the person who initiated the projection evidenced arousal in connection with the increasing closeness. These facets are so common in the stories that people tell us of invitations to collaborate and in our own experiences that they may provide us with a clear indication when a situation is ripe for an invitation to collaborate with a projection.

It is important to note, though, that the qualities that make a situation ripe for someone to issue an invitation to collaborate—increased intimacy, a growing atmosphere of warmth and safety, and an arousal of feelings among the participants—are the very same ones that may also help to make another person open and receptive and unprepared for the sudden intrusion of an invitation to collaborate. This closeness and warmth is an important natural stage in the development of a wholesome, intimate relationship. However, when people cannot support the aroused state that accompanies this stage of a relationship, the arousal may precipitate a projection, and the safe, close atmosphere that has been established may prompt the projecting person to use this closeness to gain support for the projection.

In terms of the contact and withdrawal cycle, the relationship has aroused feelings and needs within the participants, and the relationship is in what is considered the contact stage, in which the participants become more aware of themselves and the others as vivid, separate people who have the potential to connect deeply. A successful negotiation of this stage depends on each participant's ability to use his or her inner resources or the resources within the relationship to support or contain whatever is aroused until each member becomes a clearly defined, vivid individual who is then ready to merge with others in final contact. When participants do not have or cannot find the resources, either within themselves or within the relationship, then the arousal is felt to be too difficult to manage and the person may project in an effort to relieve himself or herself of the unwelcome tension. By enticing others to collaborate with the projection, the person hastens the movement toward fusion, and, if successful, receives momentary relief from the arousal. However, he or she does not receive deep satisfaction from the merging since the participants have fused prematurely before they have become distinct enough as individuals to meet one another fully and in all their complexity.

Even if we are aware that a social situation is primed for a projection and for an invitation to collaborate, we are often startled by the invitation because the content and the feelings expressed in the projection are incongruous to the climate of the immediate social situation. For instance, why the sudden angry denigration of co-workers and persons of African-American and Jewish heritage in our examples? In these cases, the persons who issued the invitation may have had a sudden arousal of feeling in relation to the invitees but may have felt insufficient support to express these feelings directly. Instead, the persons managed the arousal/support crisis by projecting. By expressing feelings of anger toward the out-group, the projecting persons were dealing indirectly with the feelings that were aroused in relation to the present transaction with the invitees. Because the purpose of the projections was to keep the feelings that were aroused out of awareness, both the initiators of the projection and the invitees were left feeling confounded, dissatisfied, and unmet in the encounter.

As our examples illustrate, invitees who do not recognize the projection or who do not realize, at the moment the invitation is issued, that the purpose of the projection is to keep feelings out of awareness will probably not experience their own arousal/support crisis as such. They will most likely engage in a defensive process in an attempt to rid themselves of their confusing heightened feelings. In such cases, both projecting persons and invitees experience too much arousal for support available and decrease their chances of regaining equilibrium or of receiving the support they seek because they direct attention away from themselves.

There are many variants of the examples we have provided. Who has not met such invitations, not once but often, not only with strangers but with family, friends, and acquaintances? Who has not felt the twinge of discomfort, whether agreeing with the projecting person or, as in the examples, being offended by her or by him? We believe that these are the kinds of encounters that play a part in the major antagonisms among religious, racial, gender, class, sexual orientation, and national groups in the world. Everyday experiences may help prepare the way for wars and economic oppression.

6

Variations in Projecting

Because the act of projecting is complex and involves several dimensions—dealing with a state of high arousal, mobilizing support, distancing, fusing, maintaining unawareness—anyone trying to contend with a person who is projecting must learn which of these dimensions is currently most important. For example, sometimes what is most prominent for the projecting person is taming the arousal, or getting rid of feelings that seem too much to bear. At other times the focus may be upon forming an in-group in the easiest possible way by creating a common enemy. Maybe getting support seems vital to the person who finds it necessary to project. Since any of these dimensions may be foreground at any given time, persons who are invited to collaborate with the projection cannot easily know what will enable a successful undoing of the projection. The invitee may well wonder, "What's going on here?" A significant problem for such an invitee, thus, is discovering more particularly what is being asked of him or of her. We think this is no simple matter. Projections are, by definition, indirect expressions and even the person who is projecting is uncertain of what he or she wants. This uncertainty makes it difficult for invitees to remain engaged with the person who is projecting without joining in the projection itself.

We have been able to delineate five ways in which a person may express a projection. In each type of projection, the person is

attempting to manage an aroused state in a different way and is
asking for a slightly different response from the invitee. In the descriptions that follow, we suggest the five possible expressions of
projection, provide examples, and indicate what the projecting
person hopes to achieve through each type of projection.

1 | 5 In a *simple projection* the individual is unburdening himself
or herself by seeing what is his or her own as something external
(Fenichel 1945, Freud 1911). It is a simple attempt to divest oneself of something that would be bothersome if it were held in
awareness as part of oneself. An example might be a spectator at
a sporting event. Many individuals live out their aggression by
watching athletes skilled in violent contact. Whether it be football,
basketball, soccer, hockey, boxing, or some similar sport, the spectator can release aggressive tension by cheering for someone who
is actively violent. Or a spectator who feels placed under unjust
authority at work may watch closely the referees in a match and
feel persecuted by decisions that presumably favor the opponent.
Attention to aggressive sports is popular among people who are
otherwise oppressed, and during the sporting event individuals
gather support for their intensity of preoccupation from others
in the crowd. And when a favored team becomes champion or wins
a crucial game, the aggression sometimes spills over into riots in
the streets—the arousal can no longer be contained within the
game setting.

2/5

     In a more elaborate projection, we see *projecting into a con-
tainer*—arousing in the other that which is intolerable within and
wanting the other to contain, manage, or digest what has been projected (Bion 1970, Catherall 1991, Hamilton 1990). A woman who
was having difficulty with her husband regularly complained to her
female neighbors in such a way that they became quite irritated with
her husband. As her neighbors became riled up, the protagonist
seemed relieved and went away contented, only to return the next
day with new stories that angered her friends. Like others who
project into a container, the woman did not confront her husband

with her anger, but deposited it in her neighbors and fostered their being containers for her projections. *3/5*

Even more elaborate is *projective identification* (Klein 1946, Meissner 1980, Ogden 1979). Projective identification is putting burdensome material in an other and then manipulating the other in an active attempt to manage what has been projected. It is common in antidemocratic hierarchies for a superior to arouse anger in subordinates whenever his or her anger is rising and the superior feels unable to control it. Instead of managing his or her own anger directly, the superior tries to handle the anger that he or she has provoked in the subordinate. Sometimes teachers may be authoritarian, and do this in the classroom—they bring up anger and resentment in students and then discipline the students in an attempt to control this anger. During the Cold War, leaders from both the United States and the Soviet Union projected their own hostile intentions upon the enemy and then spent billions of dollars preparing to control their opposite forces. *4/5*

Projection aimed at creating an in-group (Gemmill 1986, Kovel 1992, Staub 1985) is a shoring up of the distorted form of fusion. The person who is projecting is trying to fuse with in-group members in order to avoid standing alone. By being submerged in an in-group whose members are believed to be free of such feelings or thoughts, the projecting person has bolstered his or her unawareness. Adolescent gangs, commonly composed of individuals who are unclear in their individuation and who are only learning how to cooperate in new ways, typically promote such projections. Such gangs provide in-groups against other gangs and against parents. *5/5* In *projection in the service of domination* (Dicks 1967, Lichtenberg 1990, 1994, Morrison 1986) the person who is projecting is demanding that an other (for example, the invitee) introject his or her thought or feeling; or the projecting individual promotes such an introjection in the attempt to become the superior in the relationship. Persons who batter their partners commonly attribute to the partner intentions or behaviors that are said to be unacceptable.

The battered person tries to please the partner, but to no avail because what is being projected belongs to the batterer, not to the victim. Most couples who live together over long periods of time tend to alternate in projecting upon their partners. This tendency to project is heightened when the individuals are in power struggles to see who is superior or if they do not recognize the equalizing tendencies in all relationships.

passive /
aggressive

It is important to note that when projecting in the service of domination, a person may not always appear to be aggressive or domineering. Creating an image of being too weak or vulnerable to withstand disagreement is another way of dominating a relationship. With such people, the demand for introjection will have a pleading rather than a commanding tone, but by appearing weak and inferior these people often manage to get others to introject their thoughts and feelings, thereby assuming the superior role in the relationship.

Each type of projection places a different demand on the invitees. In a simple projection, the projecting person is soliciting the support of the invitees to help keep internal qualities in the external world. When projecting into a container, the projecting person is asking the invitees to manage the aroused feelings within themselves so that the person will not have to handle the arousal either within himself or herself or in the social world; the arousal is now the invitees' internal problem and the projecting person no longer needs to manage it. Through projective identification, the invitees are asked to do more than contain the projected qualities. They are expected to introject the qualities or feelings that have been projected and to bring these qualities or feelings into the dynamics of the relationship so that the projecting person can actively manipulate or control these aspects that now seem to reside within the other. By creating an in-group, the projecting person is placing a demand for unhealthy or premature fusion on the invitees so that the invitees will actively join the projecting person in placing unwanted aspects of themselves onto a targeted out-group. The demands here are similar to the demands in a simple projection except that in creating an in-group, the projecting person is asking for a deeper allegiance and a more sustained division from those who are designated as members of the out-group. Whereas simple projections may be momentary and sporadic, although certainly virulent and dangerous, in-group formations often reflect a more permanent dichotomy in the projecting person's image of the world. When a person projects in the service of domination, he or she is demanding both submission and an acknowledgment that he or she is superior in the relationship. In every invitation to collaborate with a projection there is a demand that the invitees submit to the person's needs and that the invitees cooperate without question in the person's defensive process. However, only when projection is in the service of domination is there a demand that the invitees explicitly acknowledge the superiority—in terms of either power, authority, knowledge, or even sensitivity—of the projecting person.

Although we have delineated five expressions of projections, we want to emphasize that projections are indirect messages from a person who wants to keep his or her feelings out of awareness. Therefore, it is not an easy task for the invitee to decipher what the person may be demanding of him or her through the invitation. To make matters more complicated, the invitee cannot know—he or she can only guess at the moment—what is being demanded, and these demands are not mutually exclusive. For example, at any one time, an invitee may be faced with a demand to introject, to fuse with an in-group, and to acknowledge the superiority of the projecting person. Knowing the possibilities may help invitees to gain a foothold in a relationship that seems to have gone awry. At times, this understanding may come after the event when the invitee is trying to sort out what happened. With practice, however, an awareness of what is happening in the moment may be increased and invitees may become more adept at understanding the demands that are being placed upon them and at avoiding an automatic collaboration with these demands.

Regardless of how the projection is expressed, we believe that, at bottom, the individual who is projecting is trying to regain the proper balance of arousal and support that has been disrupted. The disequilibrium can have originated either from increased arousal relative to available support or from decreased support relative to the arousal in process. Projection can be seen, accordingly, as a means of trying to regain equilibrium after something has challenged the person's more comfortable state of being. A major implication from this perspective, then, one that is most often ignored, is that further challenging the projecting person or threatening to withdraw support can be quite frightening to that person.

When we consider the intense feelings that give rise to both projections and invitations to collaborate, it is not surprising that invitees often react so strongly to the racist, sexist, or homophobic remark, which was, after all, "just a joke." And when we consider the complex intrapersonal and social conditions that prompt a projection and the even more complex conditions that are created by an invitation to collaborate, it is little wonder that invitees so often feel inadequate to respond effectively to the projecting person. The problem, however, may lie in the misguided belief that one should be able to find a simple way of handling such invitations instead of acknowledging the complex configuration of events that surround even the most casual of offensive remarks.

Once we become aware of the indirect, contradictory nature of the projection process, of how this process emerges from, rather than interrupts, the present relationship between the projecting person and the invitee, of how this process deeply affects all the participants, and of how this process may be expressed in various ways, we can understand why it is frequently so difficult for invitees to recognize what is going on and to respond effectively when they are invited to collaborate with this process.

Nevertheless, in spite of the difficulties inherent in the projection process, we would like to encourage invitees to explore effective ways of handling invitations to collaborate with projections. Good handling allows people to maintain their integrity while providing the projecting person with emotional support and the opportunity to reown the projection. Furthermore, good handling helps them to contain and integrate differences so that they no longer need to live in a world where everyone tends to create and then defend themselves against hostile out-groups.

Handling invitations to collaborate with projections is one of the many demands imposed on us in our lives. We know that there are times when other demands take precedence. What we are asking of our readers is an awareness of the choice one must make between effectively handling an invitation to collaborate with a projection and making the alternative choice of honoring some other need. Each choice has its implications and repercussions; awareness of what these consequences are makes us capable of making better choices. There are many times when anyone will make the choice to attend to another need, another demand, another responsibility, rather than the one that the projecting person is trying to impose. Yet we ask that the person making this choice be *aware* that such a decision is being made. We strive toward finding a balance between recognizing the significance and weight of the demands of everyday life and the need to attend to the seriousness and worldwide impact of ordinary, apparently innocent, prejudicial remarks. And we know that this balance is different for every individual.

Much of the opportunity for doing something lies in the fact that projections emerge from social relationships. If invitees choose not to use this opportunity, they do more than allow a friendly get-together or a family gathering to proceed smoothly. They forgo an opportunity to change those conditions that frustrate relationships with friends and family and that give rise to the animosity and strife between groups of people in the larger social world. Also, they deny themselves the chance to forge deeper connections with those present, connections that can withstand and sustain rich emotional experiences and that can help everyone to become more open to the wide variety of feelings and people in the world. With these opportunities in mind, let us now turn to Part II, in which we describe poor and good handling of invitations to collaborate with projections.

PART II

WAYS OF HANDLING PROJECTIONS

7

Poor Handling

All meaningful knowledge is for the sake of action, and all meaning-ful action for the sake of friendship.

John Macmurray (1957)

In Part I, we illustrated that invitations to collaborate with projections are made in social situations that are much more complex than they appear to be at first sight. In Part II, we examine how we can use our understanding of the complexity of these situations to respond to invitations in socially responsible, compassionate ways. Our commitment to exploring effective ways of responding stems from our belief that understanding the grounds of projection is not useful until that understanding leads to actions that work more or less well. If the analysis is so complex that people give up before trying to do something, then it has failed in its purpose. However, if people are inspired to try new ways of being when they are invited to collaborate with projections, if they are intrigued by possibility, activated to risk full engagement, encouraged to stay with experimenting longer than they thought they could, we believe that our analysis has served its purpose. Let us now turn our attention to the manner in which people respond to invitations to collaborate with projections.

Because the invitation may be serving quite diverse purposes (for example, seeking validation, wanting to dominate another, or fostering group loyalty), there can be no single response to an invitation that will always achieve the purpose of fully meeting the projecting person and enabling the undoing of the projection. Unhappily, specific steps are not available, nor are there a series of techniques we can put forth—this one for validating, this one for restricting domination, and so forth. Instead, good handling requires that the invitee, with good awareness of self and other, be willing to enter into an emotionally rich relationship with a projecting person on each occasion that an invitation is issued.

An interchange with a person who is actively projecting is always emotionally demanding and, as we have seen, invitees often readily welcome any excuse for sidestepping the matter. However, such interchanges can also be seen as ground for excitement in living. The matter is, after all, also socially stimulating: there is considerable emotion near at hand and, if even slightly nudged by the invitee, this emotion can be brought directly into the interchange. There is also ample room for creativity in such encounters, and when invitees handle a projection relatively well, they are likely to leave the encounter enriched and enlivened.

We have also learned, from our own experience as well as from examples given to us by others, that a completely good handling of an invitation to collaborate with a projection is seldom possible. The complexity that surrounds these invitations practically ensures that no one will "get it right" or respond perfectly. We view the fact that we aren't ever all-good in our handling of projections as something positive rather than negative, however, since it helps us to forgive our limitations and to stay with them until we understand them. By acknowledging our own limitations, we can learn about ourselves and our own tendencies to be racist, sexist, homophobic, classist, or simply fearful of life. This knowledge may, in turn, help us to better understand and resonate with the projecting person's tendencies to project.

All-good handling is an unrealistic expectation. Importantly, however, good enough handling is a very real possibility, for which we have guidelines to offer. Some of these guidelines come straight from our analysis of what the projecting person is about; some from clinical understandings of how to deal with projections; some from experiences we and others have had in trying to apply our ideas; some from common wisdom.

Good handling of an invitation to collaborate with a projection requires an empathic response from the invitee. In a previous study on working with victims, we described an "empathic helper" as one who can identify intimately with the victim's emotions while maintaining a clear sense of self (Gibbons et al. 1994). Like an empathic helper, an invitee responds empathically when he or she achieves a balance between supporting the projecting person and supporting his or her own sense of integrity. While good handling requires that the invitee intimately identify with the projecting person's experience, it also requires that the invitee avoid being seduced into the projection process in response to the heightened arousal. An empathic invitee will contain the feelings surrounding the projection and the invitation while not supporting the projection itself, as we will illustrate later.

Importantly, however, it is not enough for the invitee to limit his or her empathy to the projecting person. The invitee also needs to adopt a self-caring attitude. When being with a projecting person, the invitee will experience his or her own heightened emotional arousal, and he or she needs to develop a sympathetic response to this arousal. The emotions that surface in the invitee may be those that have led the invitee to make his or her own prejudiced statements or projections in the past, or they may be a function of what is going on in the transaction, as we have earlier indicated. It is necessary for the invitee to allow these feelings to surface, to be aware of them, and even to bring them into the interaction in such a way that shows the projecting person that the invitee, too, is experiencing heightened arousal and is willing to own and work with the resulting strong emotions. The invitee makes himself or herself a safe, available other by owning and managing intense feelings.

We believe these elements characterize an overriding principle of good handling: the invitee needs to respond in an empathic way to the projecting person while managing a complex inner experience. Such a response creates enough room in the relationship for the truths of all parties to be explored and respected. While this type of response focuses on the contact stage and prevents premature confluence, it also creates the ground for the unfolding of final contact, which ideally involves healthy confluence and unites the parties in friendship. This method of meeting and being with someone needs elaboration, and we will provide further thought on the matter in due course. For now, however, we intend to direct attention to common strategies that qualify as poor handling of projection and to our reasons for considering these strategies as poor handling. We believe that much can be learned from an analysis of poor handling of invitations to collaborate with projections and that these lessons can be used as starting points for developing better ways of meeting projecting persons.

Through our examples in Part I we have already demonstrated some of the forms of poor handling of invitations to collaborate with a projection, and we will have more illustrations to put forward, even when we are describing what we label as "good enough handling." What we propose to do now is to articulate a series of principles that serve as guidelines for what not to do. When we have put these guidelines before the reader, we will explore why these strategies for responding to a person who is projecting are doomed to failure. That is to say, we will attend to why these methods do not enable the projecting person to reown the projection and grow from that process and why they also do not satisfy the invitee who is using them.

We have said that poor handling results when an invitee is unable to balance the challenge of empathizing with the projecting person and maintaining a distinct separateness on the way to

fusion. In some instances of poor handling the invitee will emphasize the connection by joining the projecting person in his or her
projection, but will fail to maintain the distinct sense of self necessary to meet the other fully. In other instances, the invitee will exaggerate separateness, leaving the projecting person feeling abandoned and misunderstood or punished by an unfeeling other. We
have identified five common responses that constitute poor handling of an invitation to collaborate with a projection:

1. Confronting the projecting person;
2. Denying the projecting person's experience;
3. Withdrawing from the projecting person, either physically
   or emotionally;
4. Confirming the projection;
5. Reacting too quickly or acting out the feelings without first
   digesting and transforming these feelings.

The first three are methods of distancing, of exaggerating
the separateness between the invitee and the projecting person,
and of limiting opportunities for merging. They are methods by
which the invitee emphasizes his or her own self-definition without regard to the self-definition of the projecting person. The
fourth method consists of joining in the projection and avoiding
a full sense of self. The fifth method often leads to one of the first
four methods of poor handling; here the invitee has not given
himself or herself an opportunity to assimilate enough of what is
happening to respond productively.

One of the most common responses from invitees who wish
to defend those who are targeted or placed in an out-group by the
projecting person is to confront the person, that is, to tangle with
the projecting person, to stand over against him or her or to attempt
to have that person see the light of reason. This may be done simply by trying to reason with the projecting person, to put the "truth"
before him or her, or it may be done angrily by trying to coerce the

projecting person to adopt a more "realistic" point of view. In either case, the invitee is confronting the person who is projecting, and the typical outcome is one of ongoing debate, difference, taunting, or some other unsatisfactory opposition. The clinical wisdom that supports this guideline for what not to do suggests that "Projection never gives way to information." The practical wisdom is that the projecting person holds more stiffly to the projection and the invitee is frustrated.

The following is an example of confronting the projecting person:

> I had some friends over for dinner, and the subject of homo-
> sexuality arose. One person said that science has proven that
> it is unnatural for two same-sexed species to mate, except when
> in captivity. I said that homosexuals have existed for centuries
> and that science has identified a genetic link—people don't
> necessarily choose this, it just happens and because it happens,
> it is indeed natural. The conversation became increasingly
> more polarized.

Note in this example how the invitee and the projecting person colluded in keeping the discussion focused on theoretical specula-tions. This focus enabled the participants to ignore their emotions, even as these emotions intensified. Ultimately, they left the encoun-ter frustrated, unheard, and emotionally polarized. Confrontation did not work for either participant.

The second method of poor handling, denying the project-ing person's experience, is not only unsuccessful, it is disrespect-ful. The invitee is proclaiming himself or herself superior to the projecting person by diminishing or dismissing the latter's experi-ence. The clinical wisdom underlying this matter is "Every projec-tion contains some truth." People do not project into an empty space, but rather find something in an other that is truly there and then exaggerate or focus upon that quality to the exclusion of all else. Denying the projecting person's experience, therefore, is over-kill, throwing out the truth along with the misrepresentation.

The following is an example of denying the projecting person's experience:

> Recently I was at a family gathering and heard an anti-Semitic remark. I had been talking among a group of people, consisting mostly of family members and their husbands or boyfriends, and we were discussing how neighborhoods are not closely knit any more and that you could live next to people for years and not even "know" them. My aunt's boyfriend (who happens to be Greek), who lives with her in northern New Jersey, was mentioning how the immediate next door neighbor does not even say "Hello" in the morning to them when they pass outside their house. Then he blurted out "It's all the Jews." Everyone in the group was stunned and no one knew what to say. We all looked at him in shock but were somehow unable to speak. After a minute of this silence, one of the men said to him jokingly, "No, it's all the Greeks, wops, dagos, etc. that are causing the problem." Everyone laughed nervously at his attempt to joke away the previous anti-Semitic statement and started talking about other things to get out of the situation which was clearly uncomfortable for us.

By generalizing the anti-Semitic comment to one that attacks all ethnic groups, the respondent negated the experience of the man who made the original anti-Semitic remark. He dismissed him, denied his experience (whatever that might be, and we don't have enough information to know what that is), and closed the door to further exploration of his truth. Those who laughed along with the attempt to joke away the tension supported the denial.

Another common response, withdrawing from the person who is projecting, leaves unfinished what has been transpiring between the projecting person and the invitee, and neither one feels completed or fulfilled by the experience. As we have noted, something has been activated in the transaction between the projecting person and the invitee, something vague and not clearly revealed in the awareness of either party, and this activated force is left hanging by withdrawal.

Here is an example of withdrawing given to us by a Norwegian psychiatrist:

> I remember when I was young my grandmother talked about her feelings about black people. When she saw a black man and a white woman walking down the street, she remarked disapprovingly and with disparagement. I wanted to argue with her, but felt it would do no good, so I just listened and wondered why she felt that way.

Here we see that the young Norwegian girl and her grandmother were having very different experiences, which neither person fully communicated to the other. The young girl retreated to her own world and withdrew. While we certainly do not intend to place the responsibility of handling such a situation on a young child, this is nevertheless an example of a common and subtle form of emotional withdrawal. This is in contrast to the more dramatic physical withdrawal of the house guest, described in Part I, who abruptly departed when the neighbor complained about the unleaded paint.

While confronting, denying, and withdrawing enable the invitee to avoid collaboration with a projection, they also serve to disrupt the relationship between the projecting person and the invitee. Whenever an invitee uses one of these distancing methods of poor handling, he or she ignores something of importance that the person has brought into the relationship through the voicing of the projection. For example, if an invitee confronts a projecting person by reasoning, he or she ignores the person's affective experience while focusing on the content of the particular statement. When an invitee denies the person's experience, he or she ignores an important piece of that person's history that may have contrib-

uted to the projection. Such a response overlooks the particular
instances in the person's life that would increase the likelihood of
projecting on a particular group. When an invitee withdraws, he or
she breaks contact with the projecting person and cannot discover
what has come up that compelled the person to project. Through
confronting, denying, or withdrawing, the invitee creates a void in
the relationship that prevents the projecting person from receiving adequate support. Since we know that people who do not feel
adequately supported tend to project, this void prepares the ground
for intensification of the projecting tendency.

When we say in our discussion of the fourth method of poor
handling that the invitee must not confirm the projection itself, we
are saying that collusion with the projection benefits neither the
projecting person nor the invitee. They may have a moment of
togetherness, of confluence or fusion, but they will have lost track
of what was going on in the transaction. Since they have placed a
part of themselves in a distant other, namely, the part that is projected onto the out-group, they will not be able to meet one another
fully. It always seems easier to laugh at the sexist joke, or accept the
racist remark, in order to avoid open disagreement between the participants. Or one may simply and seriously agree with the remark
and feel uplifted by the other's expression. However, as a result of
such collusion the participants will be using faulty projections to
manage internal states. This fusion among the participants is
unlikely to produce growth and satisfaction.

Here is an example of joining in a projection given by an
African-American man:

> In law school, I often studied with a group of students of color
> (black, Latino, Asian). Our conversations frequently centered
> on the treatment we received at the hands of our professors,
> such treatment being less than fair and associated, in our
> minds, with racial and ethnic prejudice. Occasionally, we
> turned our attention to our classmates, some of whom unapolo-

getically harbored preconceptions about the intellectual competencies of students of color. Inasmuch as we were all in agreement about our circumstances as racial and ethnic minorities in a predominantly white professional school organized around a Darwinian-type ethos, we really did not challenge each other's construction of our personal experiences.

One member of the group, the Latino, Jorge, was engaged to a white woman, Meg, and she was often present at our study sessions, although she was. not a law student; she was a working woman. On several occasions, our discussions strayed into an area involving one of our members, a young black man named Alfonse. At 24, Alfonse was the youngest of our group. He was, to put it mildly, a "ladies' man." We often teased him about the way another student (an equally young, blonde, blue-eyed, very attractive woman) would flirt with him. His response was, to me, intriguing: he was not flattered at all by this particular woman's attentions. Indeed, he repeatedly referred to her as "poor white trash." Well, it seems we all agreed with his characterization, as no one disagreed publicly with his judgment. Meg was often present on these occasions, and I often wondered how she felt about our slamming of whites within our law school experience, generally, and about Alfonse's characterization of the "poor white trash." I don't know that anyone else wondered about her thoughts on the matter, but I often did; still do, occasionally.

The narrator of this example begins by setting the stage for feelings of anger and resentment on the part of his classmates—what they perceived as the racism of the professors and the white classmates. He records that members of the group did not challenge one another's construction of their experiences, thus allowing for the possibility that there were exaggerations or misinterpretations or other elements that might indicate projection going on. To further support such a conjecture, no suggestion was made that any of the participants could speak out directly to the professors or classmates to check out if an event truly was racist or was simply perceived as such. The narrator also relates a parallel remark by one of his comrades concerning "poor white trash." While he, and most of the others seemed to join in the projection (is a flirtatious girl necessarily trash?), he is unfinished with the episode and remains uncomfortable about what went on. This is especially significant because there was a white woman present, one who was romantically involved with another of the classmates present, and our narrator keeps wondering how she responded to all this. The fact that an interracial couple was present in the midst of the conversation was not attended to, and we can imagine that their presence may have stirred up something beyond the feelings raised by the professors and white classmates. Something was going on in the here and now of this group, and it was not openly acknowledged and dealt with by anyone there. Perhaps the resentment felt for the professors was sufficiently strong that some resentment of the interracial couple was subdued. But, perhaps, the students who were objects of prejudice meant also to hurt the woman in their group, who, after all, was not only white, but an outsider, a working woman rather than a law student, someone in a vulnerable position with them as they had perceived themselves to be vulnerable with their professors and white classmates. In any case, something was happening that did not surface in full awareness in the group, and the resentments were probably not fully accommodated.

Our second example of joining comes from a middle-aged African-American woman. At first glance, this woman's enjoyment of the projection appears to challenge our notion that joining leaves the invitee feeling dissatisfied and unresolved about the present situation. However, there are hints throughout the example that this situation raises issues that are unresolved for the invitee. Here is her vignette:

This incident happened in a car at my aunt's funeral in Detroit. I was riding to the graveside with an older cousin (in her 70s) and several other family members. My cousin is a professional woman, a retired college administrato:. She is verbal, spontaneous, honest and uses language well. She is comfortable with her presence. This is unlike women in my immediate family who are rather quiet and not spontaneous in social gatherings. While discussing how hard her daughter, a lawyer, was working at a law firm in North Carolina, where this part of the family is from, my cousin said "You know what it takes to please crackers . . ." or something to that effect. (Again, I try to forget.) My cousin is prone to use diminishing words; yet she is quite regal and humanistic.

I have to admit that while I was initially stunned at the freedom, the anger, and the history in her voice, there was something freeing about a woman member of my family who could speak with abandon and not have to apologize for such an "impure" thought against humanity. You see, I have been raised to try to understand when others say unkind things whatever the setting, "to rise above," to not get angry, to be silent, "it will pass," to accommodate, to fade away, as an African-American can fade away. But I do it well so it was a relief to see a woman in my family who acknowledged her racial anger, could own it. While I initially felt stunned and a little ashamed of her use of the term *crackers* to mean Southern white folks, I also felt freed, encouraged, and relieved. She was not apologetic.

And, we might add, neither was our narrator, although this is unsaid—maybe even unclear, since there is a tone of both apology and non-apology in the story. The context, a funeral, fades into the background in this story, and we might wonder if the grief that was present at the time also disappeared. But, nonetheless, our informant reports feeling enlivened by the projection upon white folks.

She experienced surprise (was "stunned") prior to the relief, as is typical of these remarks. What might be unfinished or hidden in this story? Apart from anger at white folks who are racist—a realistic anger, although the comment generalized white racism too far—is resentment against the rest of her family who have tamed her, made her nice, cautioned her into acceptance of what ought not to be accepted. On the tip of her tongue, not fully lived out and therefore not available for growth, is her anger at her family for insisting that she be nice. She notes her way of being but does not explicitly reflect a rage at being excessively tamed. The problem with this joining is that the realistic aspects of the projection obscured the woman's other unresolved issues. Whatever the case, we must be aware that joining a projection is not always simply problematic, especially when there are heavy doses of reality behind the projection.

Another example of joining a projection:

As a young teacher, I was approached one day by the principal of the school. This principal had an authoritarian style and I was intimidated by her. She told me that a psychologist wanted to consult with me about any changes in behavior that I may have noticed in a student who had recently been injured in a tragic automobile accident in which the student's mother had been killed. The principal added, "Be careful what you say to him. This psychologist has a Jewish name, so you know he's working with some underhanded Jewish lawyer who's out to make big money on this case. You know how those people are." I responded by saying, "I'll be careful of what I say."

Here the young teacher, by agreeing to be careful, took on the principal's projection. She became a temporary container for negative emotions that the principal was having difficulty managing. As a result, the principal's experience continued to be unexplored and unmet.

A mixed response of both joining and withdrawing from the projecting person is possibly the most frequent example of poor handling. In such a response, the invitee may rather weakly agree with the projecting person, and thus may join in the projection, while silently he or she feels disapproving, and thus is withdrawing from the projecting person. This strategy of being one thing on the outside and another on the inside is characteristic of people who believe they are in a weak or unsupported position in the relation ship or who fear that they will be put in such a position if they are open and direct with their point of view. Many people who have been objects of prejudicial projections adopt this strategy and when approached about doing so retort: "I have to choose my battles." Here is an example from Bell Hooks (1994):

> I then shared with the class my experience of being at a Halloween party. A new white male colleague, with whom I was chatting for the first time, went on a tirade at the mere mention of my Toni Morrison seminar, emphasizing that *Song of Solomon* was a weak rewrite of Hemingway's *For Whom the Bell Tolls*. Passionately full of disgust for Morrison, he, being a Hemingway scholar, seemed to be sharing the often-heard concern that black women writers/thinkers are just poor imitations of 'great' white men. Not wanting at that moment to launch into Unlearning Colonialism, Divesting of Racism and Sexism 101, I opted for the strategy taught to me by that in-denial-of-institutionalized-patriarchy, self-help book *Women Who Love Too Much*. I just said, "Oh!" Later, I assured him that I would read *For Whom the Bell Tolls* again to see if I would make the same connection. [p. 32]

That Bell Hooks vividly remembers this scene and feels called upon to write about it as well as to tell her class about it, shows how much that young man's comment stung her and bothered her. She was unfinished with the episode long after it took place. Her re-

sponse of "Oh!" can be interpreted to mean that she disputed with
him and meant to confront him, though, with the following comment that she would return to Hemingway's book to check it out
for herself, Hooks indicates that in fact she had joined in the projection at the party while covertly feeling anger and contempt for
this young colleague who she believed was arrogant as well as racist
and sexist.

We might be inclined to say that this way of dealing with a
projection—parties are the most frequent scene for such dealings—
is hardly a "handling" at all. It is an attempt to avoid the whole situation, whether from embarrassment, a sense of propriety at social
gatherings, fear of conflict, or other such motivation. It is as if the
invitee believes that sidestepping the matter is advisable and can
be carried out without cost. When we discuss our work in public,
we are accustomed to hearing that making a polite, noncommittal
response is the best solution our listeners can imagine. But we disagree. Overtly avoiding while covertly disagreeing is a whole pack-
age, and both the projecting person and the invitee sense the mixed
message that is present. The invitee's discomfort or disapproval is
telegraphed to the projecting person one way or another, and both
the invitee and the projecting person leave the encounter feeling
dissatisfied and unfinished with the transaction. Once the projection is entered into the relationship, the die is cast, and either poor
or good enough handling follows—there is no such thing as "not
handling" an invitation to collaborate with a projection.

Finally, to avoid poor handling, the invitee must not react too
quickly to the projection. If he or she reacts to the projection before digesting and transforming the feelings that have been aroused,
then the invitee is likely to engage in one of the other four forms
of poor handling. For instance, the invitee may confirm the projection by quickly directing onto the out-group the feelings of dislike,
contempt, or hatred of that out-group that may be stimulated by
the other's projection. Or the invitee may express the same feelings, but this time target the projecting person by belittling or sneer-

ing or in some other way distancing himself or herself from that person. Being invited to collaborate with a projection takes one by surprise, as we have suggested, and there is a ready tendency to manage the situation quickly, which often involves living out the feelings that are projected. The invitee must stay with those feelings and find a way to transform them into something that will enable him or her to meet the projecting person. An example of such a transformation is the civil rights movement. This movement took the anger that was being expressed within the oppressed African-American community and straightforwardly directed it against those representatives of society who were oppressing them rather than aggressing against each other. Unless such feelings are transformed, they are lived out in unproductive fashion.

Before we leave our description of poor handling responses, we wish to attend to the fact that no action is ever all wrong. We argued earlier that the projecting person is trying to do something of value but does it in a distorted way, thus doing something right and something wrong. (Unless we see both sides in every action we are likely to end up thinking in either/or terms, idealizing in a negative and positive way, rather than seeing all life as ambivalent and ambiguous.) Let us examine what is *right* with reasoning, denying experience, withdrawing, joining, or acting too quickly:

1. In reasoning with a projecting person, an invitee is implicitly encouraging awareness.
2. In denying the projecting person's experience, an invitee is differentiating self and other, thus dealing with the projecting person as a distinct other.
3. In withdrawing from a projecting person, an invitee is attempting to lessen the degree of arousal in the interaction that is associated with the projection.
4. In joining the projection, the invitee is merging with and providing momentary support to the projecting person.

5. In acting to manage the event quickly, an invitee is again trying to lessen the degree of arousal in the interaction.

Note that what is right about the invitee's response is helpful for the projecting person as well as for the invitee. Unfortunately, these helpful pieces are far outweighed by the unsatisfactory results of each type of poor handling.

In general, then, poor handling results when the invitee follows the projecting person in that person's attempt to divert attention from what is going on in the here and now and to direct that attention to something external. It is not easy for invitees to resist the temptation to follow the projecting person's endeavors because there is another basic ingredient involved in the projection process that makes it difficult for an invitee to connect with empathy to a person who is actively projecting. This basic ingredient is the self-hatred that has been activated in the projecting person by the arousal he or she is experiencing. An awareness and understanding of this self-hatred is necessary for any invitee who wishes to engage effectively with a projecting person. We now turn our attention to a more detailed study of self-hatred and the role that this self-hatred plays in both projections and in poor handling of these projections.

8

The Role of Self-Hatred in Projections and Poor Handling

Projection that involves hatred of another—or contempt and denunciation, or ridicule—may come from particular desires that have been aroused but that cannot be supported by the person in the sense of owning or standing behind having these desires. Qualities that are stirred up within the projecting person and that he or she is actively rejecting are projected on the other. When such a desire is stimulated, an internal rejecting force is also activated, resulting in an internal conflict of forces. The desire is met with an "anti-desire," an introject that was taken in some time in the past from some authority who had influence over the individual. Because the person introjected this earlier denunciation or condemnation instead of resolving the original conflict with the external authority in some less self-conquering way, the conflict remains unresolved. The person now feels subjugated to this condemnation, which was originally external but now has been internalized. Each arousal of the desire reactivates the conflict between desire and introject, but because both sides of the conflict now reside within the person, hatred toward either side becomes self-hatred.

When a person has not resolved such inner conflict, he or she is unable to acknowledge possession of the desire, thought, or feeling; instead, the person will perceive it as a characteristic of an other. In this case a desire (or thought or feeling) in and of itself is not too much for the person; rather, it is the desire in contest with the counteracting introject that is basic to the precipitation of a projection. An unbearable inner struggle is managed by attempting to make it once again a social struggle, a difference or conflict between the person and the object of his or her projection.

Thus, in projection, something else is going on beyond locating outside oneself a desire, thought, or feeling. The hatred, anger, contempt, or sneer that is involved in the projection is also putting onto the other the self-hatred, anger at self, and contempt for self that has been awakened. In most instances hatred of an out-group can be understood best as projected self-hatred. It is this additional characteristic of self-hatred that may account for the paradoxical situation of increased commitment to the projection when the person is confronted by others with reason, anger, withdrawal, or other modes of what we are here calling "poor handling" of the projection and the invitation to collaborate with it.

Self-hatred is not a simple matter. In some instances, the person has introjected disapproval from the authority and has taken on that disapproval as an internal guiding force. In this respect, self-hatred is hatred of the desire that has come up, as if one is now the agent of the disapproving authority. "To have this desire is bad," the person would experience if the matter were available to awareness. "You are contemptible for wanting to be dirty, lazy, promiscuous, money-grubbing, or homosexually involved." Unable to support such a want in the face of the self-negation, the person has contempt for an other who can be seen to be dirty, lazy, promiscuous, money-grubbing, or homosexual. This is hatred of one's desire, thought, or feeling that is now experienced as hatred of those qualities in the other.

In other instances, however, the desires, thoughts, or feelings arise spontaneously in the person, and the hatred that appears may support these qualities while attempting to negate the internalized

hate the desire

condemning authority. Here the situation would be: "I hate my introjects, those voices within me that demand that I disown my desires, thoughts, or feelings, and I resent being unable to live them out directly, openly, and honestly." What was originally hatred of the controlling external authority who required subjugation of those desires, thoughts, or feelings is now hatred of the internal representative of this authority, the introjects, the voice of the authority the person has taken on to resolve the social conflict by making it an internal one. In the example of the African-American woman whose cousin spoke of "crackers," we saw her hatred toward her introjected parents who insisted she always be nice. Her pleasure in her cousin's not being so nice is an affirmation of her desire to be aggressive, which she has been subduing on their authority, now an internal voice insisting she be nice or feel guilty.

Self-hatred, then, has these two faces: hatred of the desire in service of the introject and hatred of the introject in the service of the desire. In both cases, the introject, which represents a powerful authority from a past social conflict, now confounds the inner life of the person. If the person hates the desire, he or she is complying with the introject; if the person hates the introject, he or she is defying, but still giving credence to, the force of the introject. As long as the introject is prominent within the psyche of the projecting person, that individual is trapped in a conflict between the voice of the introject and his or her spontaneous nature. Poor handling fails because it does not adequately address and enable the resolution of this internal power struggle that is afflicting the projecting person.

The distancing methods of poor handling—confronting, denying, and withdrawing—fail to resolve the entanglements of self-hatred that precipitated the projection. All three methods distance the invitee from the projecting person and add the weight of that distancing to the problematic internal struggle. The invitee who withdraws, for example, removes any existing support, leaving the projecting person psychologically alone, unfinished, and puzzled by the withdrawal. The invitee who denies also undercuts support while minimizing the legitimacy of the projecting person's attempted resolution of the inner conflict. The invitee who confronts not only refuses to support the projecting person but also explicitly attacks that person's position and then demands to be introjected. When an invitee tries to reason a projecting person out of the position embodied in the projection or angrily tries to stop the projecting process or states that the projecting person is different in a negative way, he or she is implicitly insisting that the person take on a new introject. This new introject, which represents the *invitee's* authority, further complicates the internal struggle. Now the inner conflict consists not only of an established introject versus a desire but also of that old introject over against the current demand made by the invitee who wants to have this demand introjected.

In our discussions with others about invitations to collaborate with projections, we have discovered that many people believe that confrontation is the most effective way to respond to such invitations. They argue that confrontation is straightforward and honest and that it clearly conveys the message that the invitee will not collaborate with the projection. Many Jewish respondents, remembering the Holocaust and vowing not to be passive ever again, have insisted to us on the necessity of confronting directly anti-Semitic remarks, for instance. While we will note the necessity for the invitee to clearly define himself or herself, we continue to see confronting as poor handling. What these people overlook is that they are aggravating an existing internal conflict or introducing a new power struggle to a person who is already in the grip of the inner voice of an old authority. In one such discussion, a good-natured, well-intentioned psychiatrist said half jokingly, "I wish I could think of the perfect, inoffensive one-line response to racist and sexist comments so that when people make these remarks to me I could indicate that I don't agree while creating the impression that I am an all-wise, all-caring person."

Although this psychiatrist imagines a scenario where he could confront in a sensitive way, even such a mild confrontation would be an example of poor handling. Through his "one-line response," no matter how inoffensive, the psychiatrist would be seeking to impose a new introject onto the projecting person: You should believe as I believe. While the psychiatrist wishes to do so in a "wise" and "caring" way, the imposition of another "should" on the aroused person intensifies an already difficult situation. It is important to remember that the original authority who taught the projecting person to suppress desire may also have been caring and well intentioned. Those who impose introjects are not necessarily malicious; they are merely more powerful than the person who anxiously takes in the introject. When invitees confront the projecting person, they are creating a new crisis and forcing more turmoil onto an already overburdened psyche.

Joining, like distancing, also increases the projecting person's struggle with self-hatred. Although the projecting person may for a brief moment feel supported as others collaborate in the projection, this sense of support is fleeting. Joining heightens the conflict between desire and anti-desire rather than providing adequate support for the person as he or she struggles to resolve this conflict. For example, when others join the projecting person by laughing at a racist joke or agreeing with a sexist comment, they add their unaware desires to those of the person who initiated the projection. In addition, by joining the person in the defensive process of projection, they reinforce the projecting person's introjected belief that the active desire is somehow bad. Therefore, although joining initially appears to be a supportive response, it actually heightens the internal strife between desire and anti-desire by quickening both sides.

Another way of saying this is that when invitees join with the projecting person, they fuse with the person and add to that person's internal turmoil instead of remaining separate enough to support the projecting person's efforts to resolve the inner conflict. Although the person is joined, he or she is not met by an other who is grounded in his or her autonomy and who can contain the arousal until the projecting person can reown the desires. Whereas in distancing the invitee responds by going too far away, in joining the invitee responds by coming too close.

Poor handling of an invitation to collaborate in a projection is at bottom, then, a compounding of an original injustice. In the original conflict, the person was not supported as he or she tried to master a social conflict with a powerful other, and the conflict became an internal one. By projecting, the person is attempting to make the conflict once again an external one, but he or she is not supported by those present. Those invitees who distance from the projecting person through confrontation, denial, or withdrawal negate the person's unaware attempt to resolve his or her internal struggle. Those invitees who join the projecting person fuel the fires of dissonance between desire and anti-desire by adding their own unaware conflicts to that of the projecting person. In both cases, the projecting person is further burdened by the invitees' response and is left feeling unsupported in the tension between desire and anti-desire, and self-hatred persists.

Once we understand that poor handling keeps the projecting person emotionally isolated in a self-hating activity, we can better understand why such a person reacts with doubt, suspicion, or mistrust when asked to reown the feelings that led to the projection. These feelings of suspicion and mistrust are tied to the experience of being in an unsafe environment. The lack of safety associated with the quickened mistrust and suspicion comes from both the immediate social situation and from the past, at which time the person introjected from the authority what has now become a voice in self-hatred. In the here and now, the projecting person who is reowning a projection is led to deal one more time with the internal struggle of the self-hating process. Dealing with this struggle in the presence of others is threatening since one is withdrawing attention from the social relation and is vulnerable to any threat that comes from that direction. So at the moment of reowning a projection, the person must be able to trust that the environment is a safe environment and not one that will take advantage of the person's vulnerability.

Furthermore, when taking back the projection, that is, reclaiming as one's own what one has placed externally, the person is reviving the situation that resulted in introjection in the first place. He or she is bringing back to life the authority who threatened in the past and whose voice is now active within, a voice that has been treated as if it were his or her own. There is a return to the original struggle that created the self-hatred. The internal struggle that was used to resolve a frightening social difference in the past is now resuscitated and the accompanying fear or anger that was vibrating in the earlier time is now again present. In the earlier social conflict that led to introjection of the authority, the focus was on the behavior or experience of the weaker party to the exclusion of attention to the behavior or experience of the stronger one. For example, this is what happens when a parent shames a child for being careless in play and centers all attention on the child in doing so. Whether the child is unusually careless or the parent is unnerved by the child's spontaneity, the child's part is examined but the parent's is not. Focus on the child permits the parent to dominate in the situation. Accordingly, people learn that often when their experience or motivation is the prime object of attention in a social engagement, they may be vulnerable to being dominated. The mistrust, suspicion, or doubt that is now experienced reflects how unsafe the past situation felt to the person when he or she accommodated the authority by introjecting the other's command. The felt threat of the past is amplified in connection with a real threat now while one is in a vulnerable state in a social relation.

Whoever can remember deep feelings of distrusting those around one will readily testify to how painful and difficult these feelings can be. And we know from clinical experience that these are the social emotions regularly stirred up when an individual is reowning a projection. They are a major factor why most of us would rather not engage a person who is projecting in such a way that intense feelings are aroused. Or if we do engage him or her, we often do so impulsively with our own feelings at red-hot pitch, at moments when we lose control of ourselves.

Because poor handling leaves the projecting person feeling vulnerable and unsupported, it fails to create a safe environment for the undoing of a projection. Distancing and joining re-create an environment in which the person feels dominated and diminished—either by the force of the inner conflict or by the invitees themselves. Unless invitees respond in a way that respects both the projecting person and the complexity of the person's struggle with self-hatred, the person will not feel safe enough to reown what has been projected. Meeting another person respectfully under conditions of heightened arousal is not an easy task. It calls for the invitee to be aware of his or her own inner struggles and to be willing to enter into a turbulent relationship in which the invitee will need to ask for, as well as to provide, support.

As we turn our attention to those factors that prevent invitees from responding to the projecting person in a respectful, supportive manner, we see that poor handling not only fails to help the projecting person, but also reflects a problem the invitee is having. In other words, we believe that poor handling is not accidental; rather, it is motivated by the invitee's efforts to keep out of awareness or under control his or her own internal struggle that is activated by the projecting person's invitation to collaborate. As we have previously indicated, the invitee either distances from or joins with the projecting person through poor handling techniques. Both distancing and joining help the invitee to avoid awareness of or to control his or her own special internal conflict between desires and anti-desires, although each method does so differently. Poor handling is a means by which the invitee manages his or her own version of self-hatred.

When the invitee distances, he or she attempts to keep the problem located within the projecting person, thereby sidestepping the necessity of managing his or her own aroused desires and resistances to those desires. For example, when the invitee confronts the projecting person with arguments and reasons, the invitee may be attempting to keep the matter on a rational level, hoping to keep something from his or her own emotional life suppressed. The invitee's introject against unacceptable feelings may have become activated and may be working to suppress feelings or thoughts that are in danger of being stirred up in reaction to the other's projection. By telling the projecting person that he or she is homophobic or racist, the invitee is trying to impose his or her belief upon the projecting person. Meanwhile, the labeling and rationalization enables the invitee to quash some of his or her own feelings and to remain unchanged in the interaction.

Although distancing helps the invitee either to remain unaware of what is aroused in response to the projection or to avoid the inner conflict, it does not prevent the invitee from being affected by the invitation. The compulsion to distance comes up in reaction to some conflict that is activated within the invitee in response to the invitation. For example, when someone comments that "the lazy welfare recipients and illegal aliens are draining our system," the invitee may experience a number of conflictual responses. The invitation to collaborate may activate the invitee's latent hostility toward those people who are receiving free services while the invitee pays for many of these same services. Yet the invitee may also disapprove of the hostile feeling that has come up because he or she may also believe that we have a moral obligation to help those less fortunate than ourselves. The comment may provoke the invitee's frustration at not knowing which people really need help, or the comment could arouse the invitee's suspicions that he or she is a fool for supporting certain social programs. Alternatively, the comment could arouse strong feelings toward the person who issued the invitation and the invitee may experience a surge of intolerance or anger and have the impulse to fight with the projecting person. Yet the invitee may also hold the belief that one must remain polite and not disagree strongly with others in social situations. These or some other set of conflictual feelings cause turmoil for the invitee and this turmoil is what shapes his or her response.

Joining the projecting person by confirming the projection is the other method by which the invitee avoids awareness of an internal struggle. Whereas the invitee who distances frames the problem as the other's intrapersonal struggle, the invitee who joins collaborates in projecting onto an out-group and then frames the problem as a social one. By insisting that the problem resides in the social sphere and more specifically in the object of the projection, the invitee externalizes and avoids awareness of any internal conflict.

In joining, as in distancing, the invitee is also affected by the invitation to collaborate. The compulsion to join, like the compulsion to distance, is a reaction to something that has come up within the invitee. However, instead of clearly separating from the projecting person, the invitee fuses with the other and colludes in keeping unacceptable thoughts, feelings, or desires in unawareness. For example, in response to the comment about welfare recipients and illegal aliens, the invitee may collaborate with the projection in an attempt to avoid his own frustration, anger, or yearning to be taken care of by others. It is important to note that although the projecting person and the invitee are collaborators in the projection, their internal conflicts may not be the same. They join one another by using a similar defensive process to avoid managing internal tension though the ingredients that make up the tension may be quite different.

Thus, invitees who have the intention of engaging effectively with a projecting person must understand what compels them to distance or to join. The wish to avoid an internal struggle that compels the invitee to distance or join mirrors the projecting person's wish that compelled him or her to project and to issue the invitation to collaborate. By acknowledging his or her own wish to avoid inner turmoil, the invitee can better understand the projecting person's motivation and can avoid the quick and unproductive responses that briefly relieves the tension but that ultimately leaves the invitee feeling so dissatisfied.

When we examine the results of poor handling from the perspective of both the person who initiated the projection and the invitee, it becomes apparent that our list of poor handling is not a list of what one should not do but rather a description of what doesn't work for either the projecting person or the invitee. Most poor handling techniques are motivated by the invitee's introjected belief that "people should not have certain thoughts or feelings." However, we all have various—and sometimes conflicting—feelings, thoughts, and desires that need to be recognized and contained so that we can come to know and love ourselves and others instead of projecting the self-hatred that breeds hostility and alienation.

9

Three Guidelines to Good Enough Handling

As we turned our attention to what we call "good enough handling" of an invitation to collaborate with a projection, we were surprised to realize that we had been minimizing a critical positive component to the projecting person's call for collaboration. We gradually recognized that within each invitation is a search for cooperation, for a joining, for the creation of an in-group. While the surface matter is also the defining of an out-group—an other who is the object of the projection—beneath that surface is a call to communion. We can, accordingly, call these invitations to collaborate an attempt at community building. Indeed, as we noted at the very outset of our discussion, these projections most commonly happen in contexts of sociability or congeniality, such as family gatherings and other social occasions. The projecting person is acting in a circumstance that he or she feels may be supportive. Given this positive element in the invitation, we can redefine poor handling actions as either refusals to work toward community with the projecting person (the distancing form), or acquiescence in debased qualities of community (the joining form).

This striving toward community by the projecting person is a confounded one, which is why responses are so often inadequate to the quest. When the projecting person issues an invitation to collaborate, he or she is attempting to merge with others by placing differences outside the in-group that is present. At the time of the invitation, similarities and differences are sharply delineated. The projecting person is making only two choices available to the invitee: either merge and overlook differences or distance and suppress similarities.

Invitees are likely to feel pressured to accept the projecting person's divisive approach at the moment of the invitation for several reasons. First, the invitee is taken by surprise; second, there is a strong emotional component underlying the projection—the projecting person's self-hatred has been tapped and is now active in the relationship with the invitee; third, the projecting person confuses the invitee by attempting to get closer by focusing on differences; and fourth, the projecting person disturbs the natural development of the contact and withdrawal cycle by suddenly demanding final contact or fusion without a full engagement of the contact stage of the cycle. Instead of engaging in the negotiation of the contact stage, the projecting person offers the invitee an either/or choice: either we ignore our differences and merge right now around this projection or we ignore our similarities and distance from one another because we have different responses to the projection.

Given the elements of surprise, emotionality, indirect messages, and unwillingness to negotiate similarities and differences, it is understandable why the invitee is prone to accept the projecting person's dichotomous approach. The invitee is unprepared for and confused by the invitation and may not be ready with alternative ways of handling the situation.

Considering the self-hatred that has been activated in the projecting person, it is not difficult to comprehend why the projecting person wants to forgo negotiation of similarities and differences in building a tie with the invitee. In these relatively complex negotiations, each participant asserts himself or herself and becomes increasingly clearer to self and to the other. Because self-hatred is actively involved, the projecting person will have difficulty entering such negotiations with faith that he or she will be accepted by the other. The projecting person who inwardly condemns himself or herself, however unawares, is not likely to believe that others will be more accepting. Through the projection and the invitation to collaborate with that projection, the projecting person attempts to bypass the clear self-definition or self-assertion of the contact stage in order to move quickly to a phase of confluence in which individual differences are obscured.

We can summarize this part of our understanding in the following way. While the invitee typically experiences the invitation to collaborate as a threat, we now see that it can also be perceived as an opportunity. The projecting person is making a move toward community, toward deeper friendship, although he or she is not making this move in full awareness and the action involves a debased form of friendship. Any invitee interested in good handling of such moves will want to follow John Macmurray's call for "meaningful action for the sake of friendship." Using the insights from our study of the projecting process, we can say that good enough handling is informed action aimed at deeper friendship. An empathic invitee will have the overriding intention of developing a respectful understanding of the projecting person as well as an attitude of friendship with him or with her.

When we consider the configuration of feelings and motives that prompt an invitation to collaborate with a projection and the equally complex emotional reactions to such an invitation, we can understand that no simple, one-step reply to such invitations qualifies as the "correct" response. Good handling, like an invitation to collaborate, is complicated and multifaceted. Nonetheless, as we studied various responses to invitations to collaborate, we discovered that there were some common elements in those responses that we judged to be good enough handling. Building on the effectiveness of these responses, on our understanding of the ineffectiveness of poor handling techniques, and on our analysis of the participants' internal experiences, we now suggest that there are some critical components that are invariably present when handling is good. Our guidelines, again, are not step-by-step procedures; there is not a simple, sequential procedure for responding effectively. Invitees may introduce the critical components of good handling into the process at different times and in various ways. Furthermore, as the quality of handling improves, the application of these good handling components becomes more full and more complex.

The potential for good handling is created when the invitee

1. attends to the figure-making process in the here and now;
2. becomes a vivid individual in the transaction without demanding premature confluence and without distancing or withdrawing from the projecting person; and
3. supports the projecting person in creating self-definition without giving in to premature confluence in the figure-forming process.

Let us examine each of these more closely.

First, in attending to the figure-making process in the here and now, the invitee recognizes that something of significance is happening presently between the projecting person and the invitee. After all, the invitation is being issued right now, in the presence of these people, in the context of this particular gathering. Therefore, invitees engaged in good handling make the decision to occupy themselves with the current process instead of focusing on the content of the projection. The projecting person's words and attention may be directed away from the present relationship and toward an out-group, but the projecting person's act of issuing an invitation calls for the building of a unique figure or shape in the relationship between the projecting person and the invitee. In responding to the projecting person, the invitee will be developing and elaborating his or her relationship with the projecting person. The invitee who recognizes that a new figure in the relationship is being formed will also become aware of the importance of explicitly paying attention to this figure-making process instead of attending only to the content of the person's projection, since the content of the projection is most often a distraction or an indirect communication.

Attending to the figure-making process involves slowing down the process to avoid premature confluence or distancing. Thus, unlike persons engaged in poor handling who are likely to react quickly and to fuse or distance immediately, persons engaged in good handling are likely to put on the brakes so as to avoid this pitfall. By slowing down the process these invitees allow time to focus on what is happening now, as the participants relate to one another in the face of the invitation, instead of on trying to predict what the relationship will be in the future (including even a few minutes in the future). The transaction is kept in the figure-forming, developmental, or contact phase long enough for the participants to explore their similarities and differences and to define themselves. Unless that exploration takes place, the figure or gestalt that is formed will not encompass the participants in their fullness. While premature confluence or distancing may allow one or the other participant to become vivid, the resulting figure will not include a meeting of two (or more) well-defined individuals.

By focusing on themselves and their present transaction in this phase of the relationship, the participants are talking *to* one another and becoming more clear rather than obscuring themselves by talking *about* the out-group that is not present. Thus the focus is moved away from an outside third person or persons and brought back to the current interaction and relationship.

To enable the projecting person to stay with the present process, the invitee needs to make the transaction safe. Projections occur because present circumstances are creating too much arousal relative to available support. Making the transaction safe means creating a better balance between arousal and support. Without this balance, neither the projecting person nor the invitee will feel secure enough to acknowledge the intense emotions surrounding both the projection and the invitation, and they will not be able to attend to the complexity of the present transaction. One way invitees create safety is by being accepting of differences, whether these differences are in feelings, experiences, emotiveness, or social attitudes. People are defined and clarified by differences as well as by similarities, and the more clearly differences are recognized and integrated into the relationship, the less compulsion there will be for either participant to promote premature confluence or distance.

Finally, in attending to the figure-making process in the relationship, the invitee must <u>relinquish any demand that the projecting person change.</u> The invitee needs to meet the projecting person as he or she is at the present moment in their transaction. If the invitee attempts to coerce the projecting person to change, the invitee is demanding the suppression of certain feelings, thoughts, or attitudes, and is diminishing the fullness of contact in the current relationship. This is not to say that invitees cannot wish or hope for change in the other; change, however, is only a side effect of good handling that invitees hope for but cannot expect or demand. Only by sending the message that no one is required to change can all participants (projecting persons and invitees) safely and fully participate in good handling.

Whereas our <u>first guideline</u> of good handling focuses on the <u>invitee's attention to the current process</u> in the transaction between the invitee and the projecting person, our second and third guidelines focus on the participants as themselves becoming vivid individuals in the transaction. These guidelines emphasize the importance that each participant become an equal, clearly defined member of that transaction. Premature confluence and distancing are more likely to occur when one participant assumes a dominant role or when one or both of the participants remain vague figures along the path to meeting or to healthy confluence. There needs to be a clear "I" and a clear "you" in the development of a "we" in the meeting of the participants. Since the invitee is the one who is expected to respond to the invitation that the projecting person has brought into their relationship, our second and third guidelines center on what the invitee can do to foster the creation of a transaction that will lead to healthy confluence between equal, vivid individuals.

Our second guideline is that the invitee increases the possibility of good handling by becoming a vivid person while keeping the transaction in the negotiating phase. The invitee becomes more vivid by bringing into the transaction many of his or her particular attributes. The invitee's presence is characterized by a willingness to share experiences and by a sincere curiosity and openness to the other. The invitee participates in the transaction as a complex, thoughtful person engaging in a relationship that is complex and egalitarian.

We realize that some caution is called for when an invitee attempts to respond to a projection by becoming a vivid other. All too often, as we have seen in our examples of poor handling, invitees do respond in a vivid but domineering or pronounced submissive way, thereby precluding any possibility of keeping the relationship in the negotiating phase. In poor handling, invitees often become vivid by confronting the projecting person, by arguing with him or her, or by withdrawing dramatically. Each of these actions heightens the sense of inequality in the relationship. In effect, the invitee is trying to force the projecting person to submit and introject the invitee's way of seeing the world. Any feeling of equality and good fellowship is lost, and the participants find themselves split off from one another by their differences.

What we are now proposing is that the invitee make his or her presence clearly felt yet not pass judgment on the projecting person—not quicken the self-hating process—and keep the relationship moving along lines in which similarities and differences are tolerably explored. Although no exhaustive list of methods for becoming a vivid individual can be developed without limiting the creativity of invitees, we can suggest some ways that invitees may become vivid without prematurely joining or distancing from the projecting person.

When a sexist or other projective comment is raised in a social gathering, an invitee could try to expand the projecting person's awareness by showing interest in the person's experience. The invitee can become a distinct and interested "other," a noticeable listener. For example, when one of our informants innocently didn't understand an ethnic joke, she asked the jokester to explain to her the joke he had just told. Inadvertently, by expressing her genuine bewilderment, she became a vivid other to be reckoned with. In another instance, when the husband of a rabbi heard an anti-Semitic remark during an office conversation, he drew attention to himself in a friendly way by asking the commentator if she knew he was Jewish, that is, if she knew who she was talking to, who was listening to her.

In contrast to reacting to the projecting person by being a discerning listener, the invitee can become a vivid person by being proactive in the transaction. The invitee may share that part of his or her story that resonates with the projecting person's experience. Thus, the invitee may speak about his or her own experience with respect to the objects of the projection, about his or her own reactions to the projecting person in the here and now, or about his or her own feelings that have been aroused in the context surrounding the appearance of the remark that carries the projection.

We can suggest one way of being proactive by noting how an invitee might share his or her vulnerability. As we have already explained, the differences that surface in the situation are not limited to the particular social views expressed in the projection. There is also a difference in the amount of exposure each person is experiencing in the transaction. Although the projecting person is not aware of the degree of heightened arousal that led to the projection, by issuing an invitation to collaborate, he or she has indirectly asked for help in handling this arousal and is now—usually unawares—in a vulnerable position. We have learned that invitees, in response to such invitations, often also feel aroused and vulnerable; however, these invitees are still "under cover" and have a choice of whether or not to reveal their aroused condition. In poor handling, an invitee may reveal his or her own arousal, for example, in righteous indignation or increased goodwill toward out-groups, but not the corresponding feeling of vulnerability. Revelation of a sense of vulnerability along with aroused emotion can make an invitee a vivid individual in responding to an invitation to collaborate with a projection.

Thus, along with the other two guidelines for good enough handling, when the invitee becomes an open yet lively person, the groundwork is laid for the differentiation of invitee and projecting person such that the negotiation of similarities and differences may proceed and the possibility of increased intimacy may be enhanced. If the invitee has paid attention to the process of the relationship in the here and now and if the invitee has managed to come across as a vivid yet safe other, then the invitee has increased the possibility that the projecting person will feel ready to define himself or herself more clearly. Whereas in poor handling the projecting person is asked to defend himself or herself or is made to be the sole focus of the relationship, in good handling the projecting person has a chance to engage in self-definition in relation to another who is meeting him or her on an equal level.

We do not wish to give the impression that invitees are always pleasant or without firm resolve in making themselves vivid individuals as they deal with projecting persons. They may be angry or determined or in other ways quite self-assertive so long as they attend also to the equality of the relationship such that it does not deteriorate into attempts to dominate or dismiss the projecting person. In all good handling of invitations to collaborate with a projection the movement toward friendship depends on keeping the relationship alive and moving in an egalitarian direction.

Our third guideline supplements the first two and is also a necessary ingredient for good enough handling. We have suggested that, among other things, projecting persons are trying to articulate who they are, to define themselves, to assert their particularity. We have

said that they do so in a debased form when projecting—they identify themselves only as a member of an in-group against an out-group
without adequately distinguishing themselves as unique within the
in-group. When we suggest in our third guideline that the invitee
support the projecting person in creating self-definition without premature confluence in the figure-forming process, we are saying that
the invitee can upgrade the efforts of the projecting person in defining himself or herself. In other words, the invitee becomes interested
in the experience and personhood of the projecting person. Given
the self-hatred that is embodied in projections, we can define the third
guideline as one in which the invitee searches for the story of the
projecting person in such a way as to soften or alleviate that self-
hatred and thereby foster a more integrated self-definition of that
person.

There are various ways in which an invitee could implement
this guideline. For example, the invitee could overtly seek what the
projecting person is experiencing here and now, has experienced
in the past with respect to the out-group (including acknowledgment of the truths in that experience). The invitee could ask about
where the projecting person learned the idea involved in the projection, or could ask how the projecting person is now experiencing the invitee. Our examples in later chapters will show invitees
promoting self-definition in more detail than we include here, and
again we choose not to detract from the creativity of invitees by list-
ing all the possible ways an invitee can implement this guideline.

We cannot emphasize enough the importance of this third
guideline in the development of friendship and the undoing of
projecting activities. Projections involve a restriction of an individual's awareness and, since awareness is vital to the unfolding of
one's particularity and to becoming an agent among agents in
encounters, the facilitation of greater awareness is of significant
power. The best way to undo projections, as Isadore From (personal
communication, 1983) taught, is to go to the actual experience of
the person who is projecting, to affirm as much of that experience

as seems well grounded, and to invite the projecting person to listen to alternative experiences for the rest. When he believed that a client had projected upon him, From would say, "What have I said or done that enables you to believe what you are telling me?" As the client recalled the moment, From would then affirm what he considered to be true to that moment and for the remainder would offer his own experience not as the correct version but as a different version. He would then ask the client to reflect upon the different experiences of the same moment. In this way, he accepted the client's experience, he tried to foster fuller awareness, and he acted in such a way that he never shamed the client. When we began our study of meeting projecting persons, our point of departure was From's advice to build on the experience of the other. Enhancing awareness proceeds from what is already aware.

Very often when persons are projecting upon out-groups, those listeners they cast as invitees act to oppose the denigration of the out-group without attending to the experience of the projecting person and without accepting what piece may be true and may lie as the ground from which the projection has evolved. If African Americans, or Jews, or Italians tend to congregate in certain sections of a city, to create ghettos innocently by preferring to associate with those familiar to them, or if some African Americans are criminals, or some Jews loud, or some Italians antagonistic to Latinos, denial of this reality represents a denial of the projecting person's experience. Invitees may find it hard to acknowledge the frailties of groups that are discriminated against, but they must not indulge themselves in negating the experience of those in their present environment if they intend to counter projections and promote friendly connection.

In the next chapter we will expand on each of these guidelines for good handling of projections.

10

Good Handling

We begin this chapter by concentrating on one or two issues in good handling that we have been presenting, but as we proceed we will include more and more of these issues in each example because the best handling involves all of these guidelines. That is, while some good handling of invitations to collaborate with a projection demonstrate the influence of one or another of the three main guidelines, the best handling engages them all. When an invitee attends to the figure-making process in the here and now (refers to what is going on presently), supports the projecting person in creating his or her self-definition without premature confluence in that figure-forming process, and makes of himself or herself a vivid individual in the transaction without creating premature fusion or distancing from the projecting person, that invitee has found a way to move toward deeper friendship. Good enough handling of invitations quickens all of these matters.

ATTENDING TO THE HERE AND NOW

In this section we discuss the first guideline for good handling, the ways in which invitees attend to the figure-making process in the here and now. In our first example, notice how the narrator transforms the conversation from one in which the participants "talk about" an out-group to one in which they "talk to" one another.

We live in a small suburban community, about four blocks east of the traditional color line that hives off the largely African-American neighborhood. Many of our neighbors are elderly, working-class Italian and Irish Catholics who have lived in the area all their lives. Some have children who have settled in the immediate area.

One of our neighbors is a short, burly, Irish woman of about 70 who was formerly a nurse. She visits regularly up and down the street and is something of a town crier; indeed, my wife calls her 4-1-1, because if you want any information about the neighbors, you just ask or wait for her to tell you. She's very excitable, highly opinionated, and takes a grandmotherly interest in the neighborhood children, including our two. I'll call her Betty.

The house next door to us has been for sale for some time. The owner, Mary, is an 89-year-old widow who has gone to live in New Hampshire with a sister and brother-in-law. Mary was something of an older sister to Betty for 50 years, and Betty is very concerned that in her dotage, Mary is being ripped off by her sister, who, according to Betty, is only interested in cashing in the house. So Betty has been following the action on the house closely and relates the news almost daily.

One afternoon, as Betty, my wife, and I are standing in our driveway schmoozing, Betty says: "Mary's sister just wants too much for the house [a very small, two-bedroom Cape]. Everyone who's been interested immediately wants to Jew her down." Well, my wife (an Irish Catholic like Betty) glances at me, and I smile at her, and we let Betty finish her remarks, though I confess that I'm thinking about how to handle it rather than listening to Betty. When Betty finishes her point, I put my arm around her shoulder and look down into her face from beside her (I'm nearly a foot taller than Betty) and say "Betty, you're much too generous a person to use expressions like that; it doesn't flatter you." Betty knows I'm Jewish, and the implications of her speech seem just now to dawn on her. She blushes, laughs, and says, "Oh, you know, it's just a figure of speech." I squeeze her shoulder and say "Yeah, but it's not a nice figure of speech. It's like 'Chinese fire drill,' you know, it's a common expression with a lot of ugly baggage." Betty smiles and says, "Yeah, you're right; I wasn't thinking. I'm sorry." I say "I happily accept your apology for all the Jews on this block." My wife says "Are there any?" And this leads to a discussion of how the neighborhood is changing, what it used to look like, what a nice place it still is, and the remark, while not forgotten, is set aside.

In this example, Betty is talking about persons other than the narrator and his wife, persons who wish to negotiate with Mary's sister on the price of an overpriced house, to "Jew her down." In response, the narrator talks to Betty about her use of a figure of speech that touches him personally (he is Jewish) and that bothers him. He has brought Betty to encounter him directly and has changed the developing figure in the conversation. Betty is building a figure around how others try to cheat one another in real estate transactions. This is a clear instance of "talking about." Instead of following her lead and discussing these others, the narrator changes the focus in the figure from those outsiders to those in the present relationship: himself, his wife, and Betty. He and Betty are now "talking to" each other. We can notice that he has as well made himself a significant part of the figure-forming process and has been supportive of Betty's self-definition by pointing out her generosity, which she is implicitly claiming by denigrating those who try to exploit others.

We can also note relevant limitations in the response. The narrator neither discloses his own feelings or experience, nor does he pursue Betty's experience that is background to her stereotyped expression. Furthermore, he is, in some respects, calling for Betty to introject his reproach, even while he cloaks this call in soothing words. By emphasizing his height and by squeezing Betty's shoulder, the narrator may be expressing a feeling of superiority and using his superiority to coerce her to introject his position. In all probability, Betty's projection is already burdened by excessive introjects and one more will not soften that burden. Despite these limitations, the narrator has made a clear move toward friendship by engaging with Betty directly.

Slowing down the processes within the interaction is another way of enabling a focus on what is going on in the here and now. Because they are taken by surprise, most invitees lose their groundedness and ability to focus on the here and now. A sense of being inside oneself, able to stand behind one's statements without attacking the other, can be restored by an increasingly thoughtful deliberateness in the transaction. In the following example, a college teacher inadvertently discovered advantages of not responding too quickly to an invitation:

> I was sitting in my dentist's chair, with my mouth wide open and full of the instruments that dentists use when they are filling a tooth. My dentist and I have known each other for many years, and while I am quite left-wing in my politics, I know that the dentist is equally right-wing. But over the years we have been friendly to one another, I having been helped when in considerable pain by the dentist, and he seeming to find my academic style and commitment congenial.
>
> In the middle of his work, with my mouth immobilized, the dentist paused and told a racist joke to me and his dental assistant. Because I couldn't speak, I could only quietly experience the joke, which offended me but also caught me by surprise and left me wondering what to do. During the remainder of the time the dentist was working on my tooth, I considered what I might say.

As I was leaving, after the tooth was fixed, I quietly remarked that I was just then going back to the college to lead
a class on racial and ethnic issues. Without encouraging a
response, or even being open to it, I scooted from the office.
The next evening, at dinner time, the dentist called me
at my home, which he had never done before. He wanted to
apologize for the joke and said he hoped he hadn't offended
me. I was quite moved by the honest concern of my dentist
and I accepted the apology without any further comment
about his joke and expressed the wish that we would continue
to have a good relationship.

In this example, the invitee was prevented from responding
hastily to the racist joke because of the dental instruments in his
mouth. This fortunate circumstance provided him with the opportunity to slow down the process and to consider the figure that the
dentist was attempting tu form in the transaction by inviting him to
respond in some way to this joke. Instead of reacting quickly and
directly to the joke, the invitee responded by making himself a vivid,
unassertive participant in the transaction: he quietly remarked that
he teaches a class on racial and ethnic issues. Through this response,
the invitee managed to keep the transaction in the negotiation
phase and to avoid premature confluence or premature distance.
His success in doing so is evidenced by the dentist's phone call and
apology the following evening. This apology and the invitee's expressed wish for a continued relationship created the potential for
a relationship in which both participants could be well-defined
persons as they continued to interact around this matter. The dentist and the invitee took a step in the direction of community.

As we have previously stated, invitees often simultaneously do
something right and something wrong. Although this invitee clearly
defined himself by unaggressively saying that he taught a course on
racial and ethnic issues, he "scooted" from the office "without
encouraging a response or even being open to it." Such a rapid
departure could have resulted in a lasting distance in the relation-

ship since it took away the dentist's opportunity to talk to the invitee and to engage in the negotiating phase of the relationship in the here and now. Fortunately, the dentist reconnected the following evening and provided both participants with the opportunity to continue their relationship as separate but not distanced individuals.

In our next example, we see a university student making herself vivid as she responds to a homophobic comment made by friends. As the reader will see, and as is often the case, this student's better handling of an invitation to collaborate with a projection was preceded by some poorer handling. There is a turning point in the interaction: she stops talking *about* gays and lesbians as an outside, abstract group and begins talking *to* her friends about herself and her own experiences with gays and lesbians. As the invitee shares her own experiences, the focus moves away from outsiders and toward herself. The invitee who was originally only part of the background of the interaction now brings herself increasingly into the foreground.

My husband and I were visiting out-of-town friends whom we have known for a long time. In the middle of the evening a conversation began that involved homosexuals and their place in social life. My friends asserted, in a factual sort of way, that homosexual persons are more promiscuous than heterosexuals, are more flamboyant about their sexuality, and are more likely to impose their sexuality on others. They used as supporting evidence a recent St. Patrick's Day parade and the controversy about it in New York City. They were concerned about the possibility that their children might have homosexual teachers, suggesting that such teachers are not appropriately private about their sexuality and would thereby rob their children of their sexual innocence.

I tried to counter their arguments with reasoning and with facts. As the discussion went on, my friends became increasingly more adamant about their views, the tension continued to build, and the conversation began to resemble an argument between several 4-year-olds: "I did too!". . . "You did not!" . . . "I did too!"

As I participated in and watched this event unfold, I realized how important it was to me that these friends change their homophobic views. I also found the tension threatening and became aware that this discussion may have been threatening to them. At this point I decided to abandon the superficial rationality of the discussion and to talk about my experience with homophobia in the first person. I chose to reduce the emphasis on facts and to focus on my feelings associated with homosexuality and homophobia and to relate an experience I had recently had with homophobia as expressed and dealt with in a university setting. I spoke about how moved I was by the discussions from fellow students, straight and gay. I expressed some of the pain suffered by the gay and lesbian community that surfaced in a community meeting and how I became aware of their pain in a new way. As I changed, the mood in the room softened. Instead of making statements, my friends began to ask questions. For example, how did I feel about my daughter visiting friends who lived in homosexual families? I also asked questions. If it was acceptable for a straight teacher to arrive at a school social function with his or her spouse, was it acceptable for a gay or lesbian teacher to arrive at the same school social function with his or her partner? I tried to avoid accusation and to ask my questions in an exploratory way. While I know that this couple did not make a 180 degree shift in their thoughts and feelings about homosexuality, I think this discussion provoked them to ask more questions of themselves and their attitudes. Similarly, it helped me become more clear about where I stand, and my understanding and compassion for them increased.

In the initial stages of this interaction, the invitee responded to the invitation to collaborate with the projection by distancing through reasoning. The ineffectiveness of this method is clear as the argument broke down and the participants stopped listening to each other. The invitee, aware of her own discomfort and the futility of the confrontation, consciously made the choice to talk about her own experience. As she did this, she abandoned coming to a quick resolution and quit trying to change her friends. Instead, she slowed down the process and began attending to the figure-making process by talking to rather than talking about. She brought herself to the foreground by self-disclosing and by exposing herself as a participant in a process. Importantly, she did not make herself a vivid other in a superior way; rather, she expressed her own emotional involvement with the issue. Exploration of her own experience then opened the door for the projecting couple to explore theirs as well. The interaction promoted increased compassion and better mutual understanding.

These are but a few of the ways that invitees can attend to the figure-forming process in the here and now. We will see more ways in our further examples, and we trust the creativity of our readers to go beyond what we have envisioned thus far. Our purpose has been to suggest more fully what we mean by centering on the present process when invitations to collaborate with a projection are forthcoming.

THE INVITEE AS A SAFE AND VIVID OTHER

Attending to the figure-making process is not enough to create an interaction in which there is good handling. As we argued earlier, making oneself a safe and vivid individual while facilitating the projecting person's impressive self-definition are also necessary for good handling. In this chapter we use two examples to illustrate how invitees, by making themselves vivid, prepare the ground for better resolutions between invitees and projecting persons.

We believe that it is important to emphasize that not all the ways in which invitees become vivid are productive. Sometimes invitees make themselves vivid in destructive ways. To make oneself a vivid individual in a constructive way, an invitee must respond to the other in an egalitarian, nonauthoritarian, and authentic fashion. When invitees respond in a demeaning, authoritarian, or inauthentic manner, they may make themselves vivid but they are not engaging in what we call good enough handling. Many of our examples of poor handling show this limitation quite clearly.

Our next example concerns a business relationship in which the husband of a rabbi, in a few brief sentences, makes himself vivid to another person in the workplace after she makes an anti-Semitic statement.

> During his time working as a consultant to a corporation, my husband discovered that some administrative procedures were not being done right, and that a record of these procedures existed. He notified the person responsible that these procedures were incorrect and advised her of the proper procedures. Her response was, "Gee, we have been doing it this way for a long time. We could really use some Jewish lightning." My husband did a double take and said, "That's a really anti-Semitic remark." She said, "You know what I mean. This is just an expression. We'd really be better off if we didn't have these records." The next day she came up to apologize to him. She said, "I know you are Jewish and I hope you were not offended." (My husband is one of two Jews in the entire organization.) My husband said, "Thank you. Even though you did not intend to be hurtful, there is real power to words. Your words influence your children and everyone with whom you work. I appreciate that you could acknowledge what you said was inappropriate."

In this example, the rabbi's husband makes himself vivid very simply by naming the woman's statement anti-Semitic. He followed

up on this the following day when he responded to her apology
by describing why he thought her statement was not innocent. Because the description submitted to us of this incident does not
describe the tone of this conversation, it is difficult to determine
the ultimate impact the conversation had on the participants. If
the man's statements were made in a hostile, accusing, pitiful,
derogatory, or authoritarian way, the woman *may* have learned to
avoid making anti-Semitic comments, but any struggle she may be
having with self-hatred will continue. Although the man may feel
vindicated by her apology, he will not be able to trust that he has
successfully met her, and his own sense of hatred and danger in
the world will not be alleviated. If, on the other hand, the man's
tone was openly angry (though not hostile or accusing), sad and
hurt (though not pitiful), and, especially important, egalitarian,
the two will have had an experience of meaningful mutual contact with the possibility of reduced self-hatred in each. In either
case, the man has made himself vivid, someone not to be over-
looked, a particular individual (a Jewish man with opinions about
stereotypes of Jews and offhand remarks about them). He will have
evolved from a more general ground (all Jewish people) into a
particular person—a necessary condition for engaging in good
handling.

Just as paying attention to the figure-making process often
takes some time, making oneself a vivid other also occurs over time.
In our next example we see a social worker making herself worthy
of focused attention as a particular vivid person. She does this over
a time span as she negotiates a difficult interaction between herself
and her husband.

Early on Friday evening, when my husband Tom and I were
discussing our plans for the weekend, he unexpectedly made
a classist comment. As I reminded him of the neighborhood
yard sale that was scheduled for the next day, he said, with
anger and frustration in his voice, "I don't want those lowlifes

wandering around my neighborhood." His statement riled me, though I did not respond right away. I knew this was exactly the type of potentially volatile situation that, if I was not clear about what I wanted to say and needed him to hear, we would end up in an unhappy argument that would leave each of us feeling terrible.

About an hour later, after we each had been going about our business for a while and I had had a chance to sit with his comment, I realized that I was even more upset than I had originally thought. The way I was feeling reminded me of how I had felt many years ago when a discussion with my husband's uncle took on a racist tone. Tom had been very supportive of me at that time as we talked over our reactions to his uncle's racist comments in a mutually rewarding conversation. As this memory came back to me, I approached my husband saying, "What you said a little while ago about the people coming to the yard sale really upset me. I'm feeling the way I did when Uncle Ed made that racist remark, that time, remember?" He did indeed remember, and he became quite angry saying, "I'm only telling you how I feel. I can't change my feelings. You know I wouldn't say this to anybody else." While I don't remember exactly what I said in response, I do recall that I decided to let it go, and again, we moved on with the evening activities.

Tom is from a working class background, one of only a handful in his large extended family to have gone to college and the only one to have pursued and achieved postgraduate training. Tom and I share a political progressiveness and a belief in liberal causes. As Tom's way of looking at the world diverged more and more from that of his family's, he had distanced himself from them. He often talked of his fear that he is doomed to again become "like them." He still fears he, too, will spend money irresponsibly, will become obese, will say ignorant things, and will have a messed-up family life.

Still later that evening, after the kids had gone to bed, and my discomfort continued, I approached Tom one more time. The discussion began as it had ended before with his talking about how he cannot change his feelings. This time I responded by saying, "That may be true, but what I'm asking you right now is to listen to what my feelings are. What you said about the people you're expecting to come to the yard sale tomorrow upset me." We argued for a while. Tom was quite angry and visibly distressed with what he experienced as my lack of tolerance of him.

As our discussion progressed, I continued to insist that I, too, am entitled to my feelings. I explained to him that through my experiences in social work I have been going through my own process of coming to terms with and fighting my own prejudices. Now, when I see prejudice in him, it is even more distressing to me. As he continued to ask for my tolerance, he began to speak of his family background. He said that the people he would see the next day in our neighborhood would remind him of his family and would bring up his fears. I responded by acknowledging his fears. With time, most of the anger left his voice, and we were able to end the conversation feeling a sense of resolution.

In this example, the social worker first internalized her anger with her husband, then spoke to her husband of her feelings and kept on presenting herself as well as accepting him. Her affirmation of her own feelings and acceptance of her husband's led both to believe that they were important to the other, seen, heard, respected, and accepted. The ability to move beyond their anger into mutual understanding depended on each being seen as a particular person, with a particular history, and individualized needs. As the conversation progressed, the social worker became a more vivid individual and so, too, did her husband.

In terms of our guidelines, then, we can observe that while we have focused on the invitee being vivid in this example, all three of the guidelines were involved in the successful resolution of the difference between the woman and her husband. Because she came back to the matter after thinking about it and still feeling some discomfort, she made the event into one that attended to the figure-making process in the here and now. We have identified earlier that slowing down the process is an element in good handling. Here we see that extending the contact past the initial episode is another way in which to focus upon what is going on between the parties. Indeed, we have found it useful to recommend to persons who have given us examples of encounters that arose and disappeared quickly, with enduring effects, that they can return to the persons who stirred them up and continue the conversation. Persistence over time is one way in which to make an event a "present" one; that is, keeping it alive is a way of making it here and now. Accordingly, we believe our first guideline is illustrated in this couple's transaction.

The woman, insisting that her feelings must be recognized, made herself safe and vivid and thus exemplified our second guideline. Similarly, her recognition of her husband's history of coming from a working class background and having some unfinished feelings from that reality (that is, his self-hatred) meant that the woman attended to the husband's special nature and gave him support in affirming himself. She has noted that when she acknowledged his fears, his anger dissipated. Exactly!

We can point to two other ingredients in this conversation that are worth noting. First, it was not easy for the woman to pursue her concern even in this close, intimate relationship. Marriage might be thought to be one of the safest relationships in which to explore and manage such feelings and yet this couple's encounter was not simple or easy. Second, we can accept as well that there is some truth in the husband's feelings, not only his personal reactions stemming from his childhood, but the fact that these reactions came from real circumstances in his past. Every projection bears connection with some truth, and the undoing of a projection does not succeed until that truth is taken into account.

By becoming a safe and vivid other, the invitee is able to attend to some distortions in the relationship that suddenly become apparent once an invitation to collaborate is issued. In issuing the invitation, the projecting person indicates that the invitee feels like a safe person, yet this sense of safety is based on an expectation of premature confluence rather than on a realization that people can be clearly separate individuals in a safe environment. At the point at which the invitation is issued, the invitee becomes aware that his or her individuality is being obscured as the projecting person focuses attention on those outside the current relationship and wants the invitee to collude in keeping both of them vague and undifferentiated within the relationship. By refusing to cooperate in the diminishment of the current interaction and by enhancing his or her own individuality—including vulnerabilities and doubts as well as strengths—the invitee provides the projecting person with an opportunity to relate to another human being who also struggles with difficult feelings, here and now, in a safe environment.

We will illustrate further the invitee becoming a safe and vivid individual in a later chapter.

ENABLING THE PROJECTING PERSON TO EXPAND AWARENESS

We have been suggesting that individuals who project onto out-groups are defining themselves by trying to fuse with an in-group while differentiating from an out-group. They engage in this because their self-hatred is sufficiently powerful and they cannot support the feelings that have been aroused and that tap into that self-hatred. Our third guideline for good enough handling of an invitation to collaborate with a projection is directed toward enabling the pro-

jecting person to define himself or herself more benignly so that
the need to demand premature confluence decreases. Expanding
the projecting person's awareness by attending to his or her experience (past as well as present) is key to this endeavor. The next
example, given to us by a clinical social worker, illustrates the effectiveness of connecting with the experience of the projecting person.

Anna, a 70-year-old client, lives alone in an all-white, inner-
city area with a high crime rate that includes much illegal drug
activity. Anna lives in a building that has been fire-bombed
once, and she worries constantly that she will be the victim of
a violent crime. Her age, a debilitating chronic illness, and her
low income heighten her sense of vulnerability.

Recently, while telling me how frightened she was of her
neighborhood, she stated that "the hoodlums and drug addicts
on this block are as bad as the niggers." This was the second
time in our work together that Anna had used this term. Several weeks previously, in one of our initial sessions, she had
used this word when referring to a doctor who had treated her
mother. At that time, I was offended and disconcerted by her
use of this term, and because I was taken by surprise, I did not
immediately respond to her racist comment. After a few minutes, when I considered speaking about her use of this word,
I told myself that the appropriate moment had passed and that
it was more important to focus on her grief over her mother's
death than on her social attitudes. I told myself that focusing
on a social issue could distract her from her therapeutic work
and that by calling attention to her use of the term, I would
be forcing my agenda onto our work together.

When she used this word a second time, however, I decided to ask her directly about it. I said that I understood her
fear of living in the neighborhood, but that I did not understand what she was trying to tell me by using the word *nigger*
to describe the neighborhood people. Anna replied that she

had made the statement so that I would realize just how bad her situation was. "I want you to know that they are lowlife and dangerous and out to get me," she said emphatically.

"And is that your experience of black people?" I asked. "Well, some of them," she answered. "There are some good niggers, too. But they're the exceptions."

I then asked Anna to tell me about her experiences with black people. Anna immediately told me about two frightening incidents. On one occasion, when Anna was 16 and had just recently arrived in Philadelphia after running away from her home in upstate Pennsylvania, she woke up to find a black man standing at the foot of her bed with a knife in his hand. He fled when she screamed. This was Anna's first experience with a black person. On another occasion, Anna was sexually harassed for several months by a black man who was a regular customer in a diner where she worked. After she told me about these two incidents, I asked Anna if she felt the same sense of danger now, living in her neighborhood, as she did on these other two occasions. "Yes," she replied, with some irritation, "That's what I was trying to tell you."

I then told Anna that when she described her particular experiences, they did sound very frightening but that her comments about black people had not conveyed the message she intended to me since many of my experiences with African Americans have been good. I also told Anna that it made me uncomfortable to hear her use the word *nigger* since I believe that it is a derogatory, dehumanizing term. Anna looked at me in surprise and said, "Really? You think so? That's funny. Everybody I know says 'nigger.' Even some black people. There are some good niggers you know." Anna then talked about various African Americans who had been good to her and about how, on the whole, their goodness had taken her by surprise. As she started to relate these stories, she continued to use the word *nigger*. A few minutes earlier, when I had told

Anna that her use of this word made me uncomfortable, I had hoped that she would refrain from using it. This time, I asked her directly not to use the word as she talked to me since I felt that her comfort in using this word in my presence implied that I shared her concept of black people.

After Anna talked about these African Americans who had been kind to her, we discussed how her general attitude toward African Americans did not fit the entirety of her particular experiences and about how her attitude makes the world a more frightening place for her. She agreed that she had evidence to contradict her attitude but then stated that she was raised to distrust black people and couldn't help herself.

I pointed out that she had defied other family rules in her life and asserted, "There must be some other reason why you cling to your opinion of black people, even when you have proof to contradict your opinion. It must help you in some way to think that you are superior to black people and that they are out to get you." Anna then went on a tirade about the "lazy niggers" getting welfare and food stamps and various kinds of social services, while she, who had worked so hard all her life and was now in need, could not get the services she needed. This was the first time in our work together that Anna had expressed anger over her situation. "And they don't even have to ask for it, they just get everything because the government feels sorry for them. But they cheat the government anyway. They don't deserve what they get," she said. "Just like your baby brother, Jimmy, got everything and was your mother's favorite in spite of the fact that you spent the last forty years of your life taking care of her and he didn't even bother to visit her?" I asked. "Yes!" she cried and then spoke furiously about the inequity in her family.

After expressing her anger, we explored how she had lived her life feeling deprived and neglected, yet also feeling

too proud to ask for more. She explained that her one conso-
lation had been that she felt that she was better than the others
because she didn't need to ask for help. As we talked, she
began to see the parallel between her need to feel superior to
her siblings and her need to feel superior to black people. She
also acknowledged that some of her feeling of danger in response to black people was similar to her sense of danger in
response to her siblings.

Anna's attitude towards African Americans did not magi-
cally change during our session together. However, I was able
to help Anna to reown some of her projections so that we could
connect around her understandable anger and pain. My decision to address her prejudice strengthened rather than threatened our connection. Toward the end of the session, Anna
apologized for using the word *nigger*, saying she wanted to respect my feelings.

In this example, the social worker has pursued the experience
of her client and has discovered the ground on which the projection is based. There is truth as well as exaggeration in the client's
prejudice. And the exaggeration comes partly from frightening
encounters with African Americans in the past as well as unhappy
arrangements inside her family. As this ground became less background and more foreground or figural, the client was able to begin
to take back her projection and also to relate to the social worker
in a more authentic way. The social worker herself was vivid in being
open about her reactions to the use of the word *nigger*, and in her
clear interest in the experience of her client. The event also moved
toward two people talking to each other about themselves in the
here and now. The two met congenially as the client felt supported
in living out her anger and her resentment and in claiming who she
is and what she deserves.

If there is a limitation in this handling, it came earlier, when
the social worker restrained herself from attending to the issue and

also when she asked that the client not use the word *nigger* in her presence. She may have been requiring that the client introject her attitude, and the client could have accepted her request while having her self-hatred unattended. Had the social worker spoken merely of her own feelings around that word and not asked the client to change, she might have been even more productive in her work.

As a final example of good enough handling in this chapter, we share an experience that a white graduate student conversant with our theory had as a consequence of a presentation to the staff of a social service agency. We offer it because it contains elements from all three guidelines and because it shows that in a practical way these guidelines do in fact enable productive encounters. The student, Joan, was leaning on the theory contained in this work in actively promoting attention to projections and the possible undoing of some of them. She was experimenting in her everyday professional life with the application of the approach—and it was effective. Also, she was connecting with an important phenomenon that we will be exploring further in our concluding chapter. Individuals, especially those of oppressed groups, find it relatively easy to reflect upon and tell stories about how they have experienced prejudice and discrimination directed at them or at their in-group; they do not find it equally simple to reveal stories about their in-group members expressing racist, sexist, homophobic, or anti-Semitic comments in social gatherings. Jews and African Americans, for example, readily provided us with instances of experiencing anti-Semitic or racist comments; they did not as readily provide us with examples of Jews being racist or African Americans being anti-Semitic. We assume these examples exist in abundance, but we imagine that they were harder to share with us because they raised issues of loyalty to the in-group as well as issues of shame.

We invite the reader to be alert to the three guidelines and these two added considerations in following this next example. We want to underscore the role of expanded awareness for the projecting person in the undoing of a projection.

I had been working as a consultant to the staff of a small agency
for over a year and felt as though I had established a good
working relationship with the five staff members, all of whom
were African Americans, which I am not. When the director
of the agency learned of my studies in racism and other forms
of projection, she requested that I present some current theory
on dealing with racism as part of a staff training program. The
staff responded with interest and enthusiasm to the presentation, offering examples from their own histories and openly
exploring their own reactions to invitations to collaborate with
projections. As we discussed examples, I became aware that we
were concentrating more heavily on anti-Semitic or sexist examples and appeared to be avoiding racial examples. I mentioned this fact and then included an example that denigrated
African Americans. The staff nodded their heads, said they
certainly recognized such statements, and then provided a
number of examples from their own lives when they had been
the objects of projections. As we explored their reactions, I
mentioned the belief that all groups create stereotypes and
tend to project their feelings onto out-groups. I asked the
staff if they could remember any times when their family or
friends made projections onto the white race. Although the
staff members agreed with the theory, they were unable to
remember any particular examples. They openly shared comments that they made among themselves which distinguish
them from whites, but all these examples were at the expense
of African Americans, such as "Now you know, no white staff
would be in this mess!"

I was aware that none of the comments reflected negative projections upon white people, and I wondered at the lack
of such examples. Gradually, I became aware of the enormity
of my request. Although I had certainly been aware of the
sensitivity of the topic, I had not paid attention to the shift in
the relationship that such a disclosure would require. As long

as we talked about others or even about ourselves in other situations in which in-group and out-group were clearly delineated, we were safe. However, to share with me in-group comments that were directed toward an out-group of which I was a member, the staff members would have to change the stereotypical configuration of who was in and who was out. I had been asking for a new shape in our relationship without negotiating this new shape with the others.

As I called attention to the process that seemed to be going on in the meeting, several members agreed with my theory about the difficulty of shifting the relationship. The director spoke up strongly in my favor, stating that she and I had facilitated therapy groups together and that I could be trusted. However, the shift did not occur until one staff member directly asked me what it was like for me as a white woman discussing this material in the presence of five African Americans. Her sincere curiosity and straightforward question provided me with an opportunity to come forward and to share with others some of my own discomfort. Until that point, I had not been fully aware of my discomfort and I now believe that I was in some way using this material to distance myself from the encounter. After I spoke of my discomfort, as well as my basic feelings of trust for the people in the group, others, too, began to open up and share what it was like for them to be talking about this topic with a white person. As we continued to talk, we discussed our experiences in working with one another over the past year. There was a sense of play and excitement as we remembered incidents, revealed first impressions, and asked questions about one another's past. By the end of the meeting we had certainly strayed from the official topic, but an interesting shift had occurred: we had formed a new group based on our past and immediate experiences with one another rather than on the idea or wish that we should trust one another.

The following week, when I returned to the agency, one of the staff members, Tamika, told me that she had overheard an anti-white remark. "You know," she said, "I've been hearing remarks like that all my life and never thought much about them. I couldn't even think of an example last week, but when I heard this remark the other day, I thought, 'Oh, this is what Joan was talking about.'"

Although Tamika had not responded directly to the person who had made the remark, her awareness had been heightened, and in the conversation between us that followed, she and I both became more aware of some of the feelings that trigger our own projections. As I detail portions of this conversation below, note that we began the conversation talking *about* the anti-white remark and then gradually started to talk *to* one another. We discussed our own uncomfortable feelings and we supported each other by being vivid as we worked to define ourselves more clearly. As we became more clear, we were able to join each other around the feelings that lead us to project onto persons of the other's race without joining in the projection process itself. I believe that much of the success of this encounter can be traced back to the previous week's contactful encounter just described. I also believe that our ability to meet one another as equals enabled us to alternate smoothly, throughout the conversation, from being the one who was supported in undoing a projection to being the vivid individual who was providing that support. Tamika related her experience with an anti-white comment as follows:

"The other day, the district supervisor [an African-American woman] walked into the waiting room saying she needed help with carrying boxes in from her car. Three staff members went out to help her. A few minutes later, they came back carrying boxes and she walked in with her arms empty. One of the clients, an African-American woman who had been sitting in the waiting room, turned to another African-American female client and said, 'Just look at her. That supervisor thinks she's a white woman.'

"I was taken aback by the comment," Tamika said, "not because it was an unusual comment but because I recognized it as the type of comment you were talking about last week. But I was surprised by how appropriate the comment felt to me. I know exactly what that client meant."

When I asked Tamika what she thought the client meant, she talked about the supervisor's "superior ways" and her habit of asking for more help than she needs. "She acts like she's above it all and doesn't want to get her hands dirty. There's no reason why she couldn't have carried in one of those boxes herself."

With some encouragement from me, Tamika spoke about her own sense of frustration and resentment at being treated as a "lowly worker who can do the heavy work" by someone who is capable of doing some heavy work herself. Tamika then talked about how, historically, white women have been coddled and taken care of while African-American women have had to work in the fields and in the homes while not being appreciated, not even by the men of their own race. "We carry the load, but men fall all over themselves to help the white woman who isn't even doing anything. They act as if we have no feelings or emotions. White women get things done for them, but we are the ones who need some help." Tamika then commented that she and her friends often respond to one another's feminine gestures or requests for help by saying, "You think you're white."

After having said this much, Tamika became confused and stated that she felt as though something didn't make sense in her explanation of the remarks against white women. I suggested that perhaps she and her friends were talking about white women instead of dealing with their anger toward one another (as in the case with the district supervisor) or toward

African-American men, who she felt, did not appreciate her efforts. This suggestion did not clarify things for Tamika.

In an attempt to continue our exploration of such social projections and to join Tamika in her tendency to target an out-group, I mentioned to her that I had recently become aware of my tendency to project onto African-American males. "Within the past few months," I said, "I have noticed a lot of cars have license plates that are covered with a smoked plastic covering so that it is impossible to read the license from a distance. Whenever I see a car that has one of these coverings over the license plate, I get angry and assume that a young black man is driving the car. I don't like this tendency on my part, and I consciously check to see if my projection is accurate. Many times I am proven wrong, but I still find myself jumping to the same conclusion the next time." Tamika, who has had no formal training in psychology, thought for a minute and then replied, "But you are not really undoing your projection. You're checking to see who's driving the car, but you're not dealing with the feelings that you have when you assume the driver is a young black man."

"You're right," I answered. "I see those license plates and I'm angry at what I see as a blatant defiance of the law. I assume these drivers want to get away with reckless driving and that they are taunting the authorities. These feelings don't change when I see that someone other than a young African-American male is driving, but the intensity of the feeling does decrease." I then discussed with Tamika my own experience of working with young African Americans who were often angry, defiant, and disrespectful. "I think I'm still fighting some battles with them and can quickly get angry at other young African-American males." I then asked Tamika if she thought something similar happened to her in relation to white women. "No," she replied. "That's the point that seems odd. I have actually felt very much supported by white women."

Tamika then described her experience working as a truck driver and delivery person in New York City. "Many of the people who were most supportive of me were working-class white women. When they would see me driving the truck, they often smiled and gave me the 'thumbs up' sign and I felt a sense of solidarity with them. So I really don't think those comments about white women are against white women. I'm not even sure at this point that these comments mean much at all. I grew up hearing comments against white women all my life, but there was never any bitterness or resentment in the statement. I guess it's just something we say."

"So who did you hear making these comments when you were growing up?"

"My mother and the neighborhood women always called one of our neighbors, Mrs. Johnson, 'a white woman.' I grew up in a working-class neighborhood in Brooklyn and we all struggled to make ends meet. But Mrs. Johnson, who lived on the corner, dressed well and was always going on cruises and seemed to have a really easy life. The neighborhood women used to say, 'She's so white.'" Tamika paused a minute and said, "You know, I haven't thought about Mrs. Johnson for years, but now that I think about it, my mother and her friends probably were jealous of her. Who wouldn't be? Trying to raise a family and pay the bills and watching somebody else having it easy. And you know, she was uppity, like she was better than the rest of us."

"Do you think that that's what you react to in the supervisor? Is she uppity?"

"Yes. That's it, she's uppity. That's the word. And I think 'white woman' is our code word for uppity. So when we're mad at each other, we call one another white and avoid being angry and jealous of one another."

"Or at least being aware that you're angry at another African-American woman. Because you're still mad at the supervisor."

"That's right. This way, though, I let myself think I'm angry at white women and that feels okay. I was raised to stick together with other black women. So if I call her 'white,' I give myself permission to be mad and don't have to feel guilty about turning against someone I'm supposed to be supporting."

Tamika and I then spent some time agreeing that, as hardworking women, we are often jealous of other women who appear to have an easier time of it. We laughed and exchanged stories of our experiences with "uppity" women and even admitted to some fantasies of retaliation against those who don't appreciate just how wonderful we really are. Tamika and I ended our conversation by noticing that in the examples of projection that we had discussed, the trigger to project was not just a particular feeling, but the belief that we shouldn't feel this way toward this particular group of people.

One of the strengths of this example is that Joan paid attention to all three guidelines. For example, she attended to the figure-making process, in the moment, as it was evolving. The careful discussion one week around others' racist, sexist, or homophobic projections was followed by questions about one's own projections against an out-group. This in turn was followed by a working through of trust issues, which laid the groundwork for what was to happen with Tamika the next week. With Tamika, too, Joan continued to regulate the process so that contact was maintained while not rushing toward confluence. At one moment, when Tamika rejected the possibility that she and her African-American peers talk about white women to avoid dealing with their own anger toward each other, Joan maintained contact at what could have been a difficult moment by again slowing down the process; she turned the attention to herself by making herself a clear and vulnerable person who struggles with her own racist projections. A moment that could have been seen by Tamika as one in which Joan attempted to dominate her was turned into one in which Joan admitted her own weakness.

In doing so she not only made herself vivid, but she changed the process, giving Tamika the opening to express another side of herself to complete the picture she was creating for herself. Now Tamika was able to analyze some of Joan's experience with young African-American males, empowering her as an undoer of projections rather than only being a projecting person. After this exchange and some more exploration in which Joan methodically focused on understanding Tamika's experience, Tamika came to a new and more integrated understanding of herself which did include occasional anger at some African-American women. And Joan became more aware of her own anger at various groups of people.

This example, like all our examples, also carries within it some flaws. As we have seen in so many of our examples, instances of less good handling precede those of better handling. As Joan eventually recognized, her request as a white woman talking to African Americans that they look at their own antiwhite sentiments was indeed enormous. Furthermore, when doing so, she had not yet sufficiently openly identified herself as a person who also struggles with racist thoughts and feelings. It is no wonder that the trust issue came up at this point. Yet some of the beauty of this example lies with the fact that all participants continued their interaction. Thus, by not withdrawing and by continuing the process, further contact was possible.

In her interaction with Tamika, Joan may again have waited somewhat too long before identifying her own racism and attempts to overcome it, leading Tamika to hesitate before moving toward a fuller understanding. With the focus only on Tamika, the situation may have aroused too much vulnerability in Tamika for her to continue her self-exploration in Joan's presence. Joan changed the balance of this situation by speaking of her experiences with young African-American males. Finally, in her discussion of their shared jealousy of women who don't have to work as hard as they do, one wonders whether Tamika and Joan may not have been joining in a new projection focused on "uppity" women.

In such egalitarian relationships, when an invitee enables further awareness in the projecting person, the invitee is also faced with exploring his or her own experience more deeply. The revelation of one's own racism, sexism, or homophobia is never easy, and this may be another reason that invitees would rather use the methods we call poor handling than those we are proposing here. What is sauce for the goose is sauce for the gander: expanded experience goes both ways, especially when people talk to each other about themselves.

11

Two Stories

So far our analysis has focused on the dynamics within the in-group when someone issues an invitation to collaborate with a projection that is aimed at an out-group. However, as we developed our guidelines for good handling, we became aware that these principles have broader possibilities and that the target of a projection, as well as in-group invitees, can use these guidelines as a way of responding effectively to a projection. Our first story comes from a target of a series of virulent attacks.

For a projection to serve its purpose, the object of that projection must remain distant and vague enough to accommodate the various qualities that the projecting person puts onto him or her or the group. However, by attending to the here and now, by refusing to cooperate in remaining distant and vague, and by fostering awareness in the projecting person, the target of a projection may decrease the possibility that the projection will "take," and may increase the possibility that the projecting person may reown whatever has been projected.

We suspect that many of our readers may be skeptical about the effectiveness of such a response by the object of a projection or may wonder why someone who has been relegated to the out-group would want to invest so much energy and effort into implementing any guideline for establishing a relationship with someone who is using him or her as an object of a hostile projection. To those who are indeed skeptical, we suggest that because the projecting person is dependent on the object of the projection to carry the split-off feelings, a relationship already exists. By acknowledging its existence and by becoming actively involved in negotiating the relationship, the targeted person may not only decrease the hostility and the sense of danger that both participants in the relationship feel, but may also create the possibility of turning this already deeply charged relationship into one that is emotionally satisfying for all involved. Ignoring the fact of a relationship is a form of denial that is socially dangerous.

To illustrate how acknowledging the connection and responding in friendship can transform the lives of those involved in a social projection, we would like to refer to Kathryn Watterson's book, *Not by the Sword* (1995). In this book, which is an account of a true story, Watterson describes how a Jew, Cantor Michael Weisser, and his wife Julie responded to threats from Larry Trapp, then the Grand Dragon of Nebraska's Ku Klux Klan. Instead of following the advice of police and friends who warned them to keep away from Trapp, the Weissers actively made themselves known to Trapp. They acted on the belief that there was more to Trapp than the hate he espoused, and they gradually encouraged him to address his own vulnerability and wish for ties to others. As their relationship slowly developed, Trapp and the Weissers became close friends, with Trapp eventually converting to Judaism and with the Weissers inviting the terminally ill man to move into their home where he spent the last months of his life. Although most of us are not prepared to establish the kind of intimate relationship that this couple established with the Klansman, the Weissers' response highlights the possibilities available for meaningful contact when people are willing to remain open to negotiating a relationship with a person who is using them as an object of a negative projection.

Michael and Julie Weisser first became aware that they were being targeted by Trapp when they received a threatening phone call soon after moving into their new home in Lincoln, Nebraska: "The man's voice on the other end of the line—startlingly harsh and hateful—seemed loud as he pronounced each word distinctly: 'You *will be sorry* you ever moved into 5810 Randolph Street, Jew boy'" (p. 25). Two days later, the Weissers received a packet of hate mail, containing circulars and pamphlets with dehumanizing caricatures of Jews and blacks, "facts" asserting that the Holocaust never happened, and threats to the welfare of anyone who wasn't a white Aryan Christian. Also included in this packet were handwritten messages to the Weissers. One stated that "'The KKK is watching you, Scum'" and another stated that "'The "Holohoax" was nothing compared to what's going to happen to you!'" (p. 39).

When the Weissers reported these incidents to the police, they were told that the threats were probably coming from Larry Trapp, the head of the state's KKK who led a group of skinheads and Klansmen terrorizing black, Asian, and Jewish families in Nebraska and Iowa. The police warned the Weissers that Trapp was a dangerous man who made explosives in his apartment and who was suspected of firebombing several homes and of burning an Indochinese refugee center in Omaha.

Although they were advised to stay away from Trapp, both Julie and Michael found themselves drawn to respond to him. Julie considered sending him a letter and a different proverb every day in order to teach him how to treat his fellow man. When she mentioned this plan to Michael, he became concerned for her welfare and asked her to send these letters anonymously. "'No,'" she replied. "'I want him to know who it's from. He's the one who does things anonymously'" (p. 102). Although she did not send these letters, Julie found herself thinking often about the man who was threatening her and her family, and she started driving by his apartment every time she went into town. Julie explained, "'Something kept motivating me to drive by. . . . I was not only curious but I had the sense there was more to Larry than what had been presented in the newspapers or on television'" (p. 101).

The Weissers' response here and later in this example suggests that they were intuitively aware of what we have called the guidelines of good handling. They recognized that Trapp was creating a significant relationship with them even though his intention was to distance himself from them by making them the objects of his projections. From the beginning, the Weissers attended to the figure-making process of this relationship and became actively involved in helping to create the shape or form that unfolded in it. Although they did not start out deciding to befriend Trapp, they paid attention to the here and now at each step of the process, beginning with some vague sense of being "drawn to respond to him." They did not insist that Trapp change or that the relationship take a certain shape. Over a period of months, they continued this process of acknowledging how they were experiencing the current relationship while expressing their belief that something better was possible.

The Weissers also moved toward becoming vivid actors in the transaction early on. Julie's refusal to send the notes anonymously indicates her refusal to remain an undefined, stereotypical figure. Just as she sensed that there was more to Larry than what had been presented by the media, she also wished him to see her as more than some opaque, distant object who was willing to collude in keeping the particularity and vividness of each person out of the relationship. Although Julie did not act on her wishes—and perhaps wisely so, considering Trapp's police record for harassment—her inclinations kept her open and receptive for future opportunities to respond effectively to Trapp. And later, when Michael responded to Trapp, he was willing to bring his whole experience into the relationship: his anger, confusion, and frustration as well as his hope for something better.

As we will see, the Weissers were also willing to support Trapp as he defined himself with them. It is important to note that the Weissers did not arbitrarily decide that Trapp was a pained, vulnerable person who needed their love. To do so would have been to respond to his projection with projections of their own, projections that would have carried a sense of superiority. Instead, they remained open to the possibility that Trapp *could* be vulnerable and in need of support as well as remaining aware that he often was infuriating and dangerous. Julie's decision not to send signed notes to Trapp indicates her realistic sense that Trapp could be dangerous. As we describe later in this chapter, Michael's willingness to remain connected with Trapp while responding directly to Trapp's infuriating actions provided Trapp with a supportive relationship within which he could begin to assert and define himself more fully. Michael's strong, honest reactions helped Trapp to see himself more clearly and to see Michael as someone who could acknowledge aroused emotion while staying in the relationship with an other. Michael's offer of friendship provided Trapp with a safety net as he began to explore his self-hatred and his wishes for acceptance and love.

As we continue to examine the Weissers' relationship with Trapp, we will note more specifically how the Weissers' effective handling of Trapp's projections helped to create a lively, yet safe enough, interdependence in which all parties were able to define themselves vividly and to reveal deep truths about themselves.

When Trapp sponsored a white supremacist television series on a local cable channel, Michael Weisser became furious and told Julie he had to call Trapp. Then, when Michael did call, he heard an eleven-minute-long, vicious tirade against blacks and women on Trapp's answering machine. For weeks, Michael called Trapp's number, waited for the sound of the beep after the latest hate message, and left his own message for Trapp. Once he said, "'Why do you hate me? You don't even know me, so how can you hate me?'" (p. 119). Another time, after seeing Trapp interviewed in his wheelchair on a television show, Michael left the following message:

"Larry, I just saw an interview with you in your Klan getup in front of the Nazi flag. Larry, do you know that the very first

laws Hitler's Nazis passed were against people like yourself who
had no legs or who had physical deformities, physical handi-
caps? Do you realize you would have been among the first
to die under Hitler? Why do you love the Nazis so much?"
[p. 121]

Without identifying himself by name, Weisser was bringing to
Trapp's consciousness the possibility that Trapp's hatred was based
on his lack of awareness of the particular characteristics that defined
both the objects of his projection and himself. Trapp's hatred of
Weisser was easy since he did not know him, and his allegiance to
the Nazis was predicated on his denial that his disabilities would have
made him a victim of their laws. By trying to make both himself and
Trapp more vivid and particular, Weisser was attempting to change
the stereotyped, polarized relationship between Jews and the Ku
Klux Klan to a more individualized connection between two clearly
defined human beings.

Michael Weisser did not attempt to keep the anger and frustration out of his voice as he left messages for Trapp. By letting Trapp
know that he was personally affected by Trapp's campaign, Weisser
was calling Trapp's attention to the fact that he, Michael Weisser, a
Jew, was a real person with whom Trapp had created a relationship
by projecting onto him. Their relationship, as it stood, was certainly
not a pleasant one. However, Weisser was beginning to negotiate a
better relationship by making Trapp acutely aware of the unpleas-
antness of their current connection and by providing Trapp with
an opportunity to see at least one Jewish person as a vivid rather
than as a distant, vague individual. Coupled with an expression of
his anger and frustration, Weisser extended an offer of friendship
to Larry, indicating that their uncomfortable relationship need not
always be unpleasant. At one point, Weisser left a message promis-
ing a possibility of love when Trapp gave up his hatred.

Although Weisser willingly made himself a clearly defined
person to Trapp and spoke in general terms about having a better

relationship (though he remained nameless), he had no idea what
he would do if Trapp ever responded to him. When Michael asked
Julie what he should do if Larry picked up the phone while he was
leaving a message, Julie suggested that Michael offer to do something nice for him. "'Tell him you'll take him to the grocery store
or something like that'" (p. 124). Julie also told Michael that often
as she drove by Larry's apartment she was struck by how lonely he
must be, how isolated in all his hatred. To her, it seemed obvious
that "'a man so filled with malice was missing the ingredient of love
in his life'" (p. 124). This, of course, was her projection since she
could not have known whether he was lonely or full of loving friendships within his in-group.

Julie's suggestion of helping Trapp with his grocery shopping
reflected an awareness of the importance of responding to the
uniqueness of the person who is projecting. Such an offer would
indicate that they saw Trapp as a person with his own particular
nature and needs and would convey the idea that they were willing
to respond in friendship to him as they saw him.

After several months of phone calls, Trapp did finally respond.
As Michael was leaving a message, Trapp grabbed the phone and
said, "'What the fuck d'you want?' Michael replied, 'I just want to
talk to you.'" Trapp threatened to have Michael arrested for harassing him: "'Why the fuck are you harassing me?! Stop harassing
me! . . . What do you want?'" Remembering Julie's advice, Michael
said, "'Well, I was thinking you might need a hand with something
and I wondered if I could help. I know you're in a wheelchair and
I thought maybe I could take you to the grocery store or something'"
(p. 144). After a moment of silence, Trapp cleared his throat and
when he spoke his voice sounded different to Michael Weisser.
Michael felt certain that he heard the texture of Larry's voice soften
and lose its edge of hatred. "'That's okay,' Larry Trapp said. 'That's
nice of you but I've already got that covered. Thanks anyway. But
don't call this number anymore.'" Before Trapp could hang up,
Michael Weisser said, "'I'll be in touch'" (p. 144).

According to Watterson, this first conversation between Weisser and Trapp changed Weisser's perspective on Trapp: Michael's "initial response to Trapp's hatred had been fueled by anger and a desire to fight back, but since their first exchange, he'd started thinking of Larry Trapp as a destructive but vulnerable, messed-up person who needed a new perspective on the world" (p. 147). Michael now began to wonder if he and Trapp had experienced similar difficulties as children. Michael suspected that Trapp, like himself, had been abused as a child and had, as a teenager, been in trouble with the law. The possibility of these similarities (a projection that Michael was eventually able to check out and confirm with Trapp) helped Michael to be more empathic with Trapp and to recognize that much of Trapp's hatred originated in the injustices and pain associated with his earlier life. Unlike Michael, Trapp had not had supportive people in his youth and so he remained isolated with this anger and pain until he found organizations like the KKK and the Nazi party to give him the illusion of power, belonging, and strength. By identifying with these groups, Trapp had attempted to divest himself of his undesirable qualities and by joining these organizations he bolstered the projection of his own fears, self-hatred, and vulnerability onto others. By refusing to validate these projections—either by accepting them passively or remaining polarized and reacting to Trapp as "the enemy"—the Weissers were eventually able to help and support Trapp in reowning these projections and tolerating his anger, fears, and pain.

It is important to remember that as he responded to Trapp, Michael Weisser did not suppress his anger in order to be some magnanimous influence in Trapp's life. By avoiding his anger, Michael would have become unreal and untrustworthy. Instead, by bringing his anger openly into his conversations he made Trapp aware of how profoundly Trapp's actions were affecting this particular Jewish man. It was only by expressing his anger and by remaining in the relationship as an angry person who was willing to reach out toward friendship that Weisser was able to connect on an honest level with Trapp. Although Michael and Julie were prepared to offer help to Trapp, they were also willing to keep the relationship with Trapp in the initial unpleasant stage until Trapp indicated that he was open to talking (his picking up the phone and his question, "'What do you want?'"). Although Julie had quickly suspected that Trapp was a lonely, unhappy man, she also recognized his dangerous aspects and was willing to contain her desire to help until Trapp asked for assistance. This request did not come until months after Trapp's first threatening phone call.

In November, Michael Weisser read in the local paper that Trapp was taking his show "Race and Reason" off the air. Michael called Trapp to discuss Trapp's apparent change of heart, but Trapp emphatically replied that he was not having a change of heart and that he was still a Klansman and a Nazi.

A few nights later, Larry surprised Michael by calling and saying, "'I want to get out, but I don't know how'" (p. 159). Responding to Larry's conflict, Michael suggested that he and Julie meet Trapp at his apartment to discuss Trapp's dilemma. Julie decided that she wanted to give Larry a gift, and she chose a silver ring of intertwined strands she had bought for Michael several years earlier. Julie and Michael thought that this was a perfect gift because the ring was twisted but beautiful, just as a person's life could be both twisted and beautiful.

What the Weissers didn't know at this point was that the gift of the ring was especially appropriate since Larry's swastika rings had begun feeling heavy and uncomfortable the night before and that his ring fingers had begun to itch and burn as he thought about how he wanted to change his life.

Feeling both excited and apprehensive, Michael and Julie knocked at Trapp's apartment door:

The door creaked open slowly and Michael and Julie saw the bearded Larry Trapp in his wheelchair. An automatic weapon— a MAC 10—was slung over the door knob on the back of the door and a huge Nazi flag hung on the wall behind him. . . .

> Michael walked over and took Larry's outstretched hand in his and said, "It's good to really meet you in person." At the touch of Michael's warm, strong hand, Larry winced as if he had been hit by a jolt of electricity. Then he broke into tears.
>   He didn't know what had hit him, but he looked down and began yanking at the two silver swastika rings on his fingers. He clumsily pulled one off and pulled off the other and held them out in the palm of his hand. "Here, I can't wear these anymore," he said, beginning to cry even harder. "I want you to take these rings. They stand for all the hatred in my life. Will you take them away?" [pp.164–165]

Michael and Julie took the rings and then presented Trapp with their gift. Trapp looked at the ring they had offered him in friendship and then apologized for all the harm he had done. That night, Michael, Julie, and Larry talked for three hours. Larry told them he wanted to quit the Klan, quit the Nazi party, quit racism, and try to make up for all the terrible things he had done.

Larry spent the next few days calling his contacts in the KKK and the Nazi party and explaining his reasons for leaving these organizations. He also called people he had personally hurt or harassed and apologized to them. He contacted the FBI, telling them he would cooperate with their investigation into the KKK's and the Nazi Party's illegal activities, and he sent a letter to all the news media, apologizing for the abusive language and derogatory comments he had made about the various minority groups in the area.

During the following months, the friendship between Trapp and the Weissers grew, with the Weissers introducing Trapp to their children and including him in family activities. Michael fostered an equal, respectful relationship by revealing to Trapp many of his own early experiences of neglect and abuse and his own brushes with the law as a teenager. "'We're not as different from each other as you think'" (p. 200), Michael told Larry, even though they had taken very different paths in life.

At the end of December 1991, Larry was told by his doctors that he had less than a year to live. Within a few days, the Weissers invited Larry to move into their home. Larry lived with them for most of the next year, becoming a part of their family, converting to Judaism, and, as long as he was physically able, giving talks at juvenile detention centers about his own experiences in order to illustrate the dangers of hatred.

As Larry's condition deteriorated, Julie resigned from her job as a nurse to care for him. Larry died on September 6, 1992. Before his death, Larry commented that

"God touched my life. I thought I was a Christian and this, that, and the other, but God really came into my life through a messenger—Michael Weisser. Through the love he extended to me, just our phone conversations, I could feel the love in his voice. I didn't know how to act. He was a shock to me." [p. 252]

The story of the Weissers and Larry Trapp is certainly a profoundly moving, extraordinary story of people's ability to transcend hatred. By making themselves vivid and by continuing to relate to Trapp in an honest, energetic way, the Weissers were able to help shape their relationship with Trapp so that they were safe enough for him to depend on to support him as he began to reown and undo his self-hatred. By giving Larry the time and space to participate as an equal and negotiate their relationship—instead of demanding that he conform within a short period of time to their concept of how he must be—the Weissers provided Larry with a context in which to grow and discover his potential for love. If the Weissers had insisted that Larry change, and if they had been successful, at best they may have succeeded in stopping his harassment of them. His self-hatred, however, would merely have been diverted, and another group—or possibly Larry himself—would have become the target. Instead, the Weissers were able to create an environment that provided Trapp with the opportunity both to undo his self-hatred and to define himself according to his basic truth within the context of a caring relationship, an opportunity that had been sorely lacking in Trapp's life.

Trapp himself came to understand the role that self-hatred played in the organizations to which he had belonged: "'They're confused people, the Klan and the Nazi Party; they're—I think they really hate themselves is what their problem is. They don't want to punish themselves, so they want to try to punish someone else. Basically, I think that's what the problem is'" (p. 252).

Through their offer of friendship, the Weissers provided Trapp with a pathway out of the self-hatred he was projecting onto others. No one could have predicted—not even Trapp himself—the dramatic change that the Weissers' offer of friendship effected in Trapp. And much of this change was a result of no one's insisting that he conform to a certain image. When Larry began to change, he broke the mold, transcending a life of pain and hatred, learning to love and showing others how to love. After Trapp's death, Julie Weisser acknowledged that Trapp had given them as much as they had given to him.

Although the story of the Weissers and Trapp is inspiring, it may also provide us with another key as to why we are so often reluctant to respond in a lively way to projections and to invitations to collaborate with projections. Most of us are not prepared to invest so much of ourselves and our lives into the lives of others. If responding in friendship can lead to the type of intimate relationship that the Weissers had with Trapp, then aren't we wise to avoid responding to every offhand, casual projection? How many relationships are we capable of or even interested in having?

In response to such questions, we would refer the reader back to our first guideline for good handling. In this guideline, we discuss the importance of negotiating the shape or form of the relationship in the here and now. The Weissers were not obliged to become so intimately connected with Trapp, just as Trapp was not obligated to accept their overtures of friendship. The participants in this relationship negotiated each stage of their developing connection, making conscious choices about how involved they wanted to be. If the Weissers had stopped at any stage in the relationship, they would still have engaged in good handling. What is fortunate is that they remained engaged with Trapp and provided themselves and Trapp with enough space and nurturance in the relationship to allow a loving, respectful friendship to blossom. This friendship stands as a testament to the possibilities that emerge when we respond in friendship to projecting persons.

Responding to prejudice and projections in a way that encompasses all three of our guidelines for good handling does not require the extraordinary efforts that the Weissers went through in our previous example. We admire and respect all that the Weissers were able to do and, in focusing on the ordinary experiences of everyday life, our main interest is in exploring and discovering what any one of us might be able to do when faced with a particular projection in any given moment. Furthermore, we remind the reader that when the Weissers initially responded to Trapp's threats and hate mail, they did not, and could not, foresee how far they were willing to go in their interactions with him. Through her description of the Weissers' responses to Trapp's projections, Kathryn Watterson does not simply describe one incident; she describes many events with each response building on the previous one. Our lives and relationships also consist of many episodes; our response to someone today is the ground for tomorrow's interaction. We do not know how good handling today will shape our interactions tomorrow, and that is not our primary concern. Instead, our interest is with how to handle an invitation to collaborate with a projection in the here and now, at this moment.

Our second story refers to a climactic event that took place over a fairly short period of time. It occurred one evening at the home of a person who on many previous occasions had issued invitations to collaborate with projections aimed at minority groups. As we have seen repeatedly in our previous examples, the episode of good handling was preceded by poor handling. Past invitations to collaborate with projections by the projecting person had resulted over and over in withdrawal by the invitee. The invitee's continued discomfort prepared the ground for good handling. With minor editing, we present the following story as Laura Cohen wrote it for us.

THE STRANGER

"Well, all I can say is that I think Jason would be receptive if you talked to him. Aside from that, I guess I'm out of suggestions for you," Wil said with a sigh. It was one of those sighs that meant he was angry and frustrated, yet struggling his hardest to end this discussion in a diplomatic way. My partner Wil and I had been through this discussion so many times before, and I realized once again that I was taking his patience for granted. I knew I was being unfair to him by talking with such hostility about his only brother, Jason. Yet after a year of living with Wil in Buffalo, two miles away from Jason and his wife, I still hadn't found a way to express to Jason how much his racist, classist, and homophobic attitudes upset me.

"I don't know," I said. "I keep telling myself that I'll call him on it sometime soon, but then once he gets started on a rampage against a group of people, it's impossible to get a word in edgewise. You know how he is once he gets going." I was also afraid to "rock the boat." I had never before confronted anyone in Wil's family, besides Wil, about anything. I wasn't sure what the code of conduct was. Furthermore, I had never seen anyone confront Jason about anything. He could be intimidating at times. Therefore, in the past year, I had held it in, biting my tongue at barbecues, concerts, family dinners, and frequent evening get-togethers with Jason and his wife.

The hardest part was work. Jason had gotten me a job at the small company he worked for, so I spent most of my weekdays in a tiny office with him, where he and our other co-worker, Alvin, kept the radio tuned to a talk radio program hosted by a man named J. R. Gash. J. R.'s claim to fame was that he was the man whom Rush Limbaugh had learned from. In fact, the popular consensus in Buffalo was that J. R. was even more conservative and blatantly prejudiced than Limbaugh himself. I remember my days in that office like time spent in a torture chamber.

Wil assured me, as he had numerous times, of what a genuinely warm, caring person Jason was. "You have to understand," Wil explained, "Jason's from a small, conservative rural town. We didn't interact with anyone but white Protestants and Catholics in Bellsville. Jason hasn't had many experiences with minorities." "So what?" I replied. "Wil, you're from the same home town as your brother, and you are not a racist. That's no excuse. It's his responsibility to not remain ignorant and to not judge all these people he's never even come into contact with."

The argument then dropped off into silence. It was unfair of me to expect Wil to revoke his loyalties to his brother, with whom he was very close. This was my battle and I would have to fight it on my own, somehow. This particular argument, on a rainy March evening, filled me with a greater sense of urgency to resolve the situation. I saw that I couldn't continue to pressure Wil, and I knew that I was unable to keep my frustrations to myself.

The next day at work was a usual day of J. R.'s morning radio program accompanied by a few chuckles and remarks from Jason and Alvin. I got home by five o'clock, took a deep breath, and dialed Jason's number. I asked Jason if I could come over to talk to him because I was having a problem, and I thought he might be able to help me with it. Jason immediately said, "Sure, come on over. I'll do whatever I can."

As I drove the now too-short distance to his house, my heart was a cement block in my chest and my fingers were stiff and ice-cold around the steering wheel. I wished the ride was longer. As I took a couple of deep breaths, I realized for perhaps the first time all day that tonight was the first night of Passover. Being unable to make it home to Philadelphia for most Jewish holidays that year had only made me feel more removed from my own culture. In the past few weeks, I had seen no reminders that my favorite holiday was right around the corner. Now I felt like I had wandered so far from my own shore that I had gone completely undercover, even to myself. Once I realized how hollow that felt, I was overcome with a surge of emotion. I had arrived at another Passover, the holiday that symbolizes to me an appreciation for the close ties that we have and our freedom to be who we are and to honor our past without hiding. This year, I was spending it alone without performing even one token ritual.

I thought about the one lesson from the story of Passover that I believe is the most important. It is the admonishment to never turn away a stranger. It says that as strangers in Egypt, we as Jews know the suffering and sorrow of having been cast out in foreign, hostile land. Therefore, as a Jew, you should never turn your back on a stranger, because you know the stranger, you are the stranger. Therefore, always welcome them, meet them, and offer of yourself. Suddenly, as I drove, this message became stronger than anything else, and I felt a power surge of adrenaline. My hands started to warm up. I saw that I was not plunging myself into an icy chasm by confronting Jason. I was forging ahead to resolve something that affected me at a very deep level. It went beyond the fact that Jason's attitude infuriated me. It was more than the fact that his scapegoating onto minorities threatened me because it brought up my own old feelings of being the underdog. It was more than being fair to Wil, and honoring his loyalty to his only brother. It was broader, larger, more profound, this disturbance that I had to settle. Yet although it went beyond my individual life circumstances in the present, it was very specific and very necessary. I felt it at the core, not only of who I am in my immediate life, but also of my place and peace in the world.

I realized that I was not going to talk to Jason for the sole purpose of protecting and defending the groups he had targeted with his racism. I knew I couldn't change his views with a conversation, and I didn't expect to do so. At that moment, those minorities were not "the stranger" that I was seeking to meet. The stranger, I realized, was Jason. Jason was the stranger because I had made myself a stranger to him. I had done this by holding myself back all this time and letting the pain of his remarks build up into mountains of anger and hatred that felt bigger than myself. I had distanced myself from him, revealing only minor parts of who I am that were unrelated to what was truly affecting me. I had deceived him by "playing nice" and hiding my true self and what was meaningful to me. I was living a very big lie. I had not given of myself, and I do not mean "give" in the altruistic, selfless sense. I mean that if I had told him what was upsetting me and what I would not tolerate and why, and also how important our relationship was to me, I would have been telling Jason who I am. I would have been giving of my true self. But instead, I had pretended to him that everything was fine, while I secretly let my hostility build to such heights that my empathy for him as a human being had begun to dwindle. In the privacy of my own mind and heart, I had treated him as an evil villain, as if he had no feelings or compassion. This is how I had alienated myself from Jason and had made him a stranger. I had made myself a stranger to him.

As I pulled into Jason's driveway, I decided that this conversation would be as appropriate a way to usher in the first night of Passover as any other. We sat down in the living room, and I took a deep breath. I began the conversation by telling him that there was something going on that was making me uncomfortable. I said that I wanted to talk to him about it because I thought that perhaps he could help me with it. Jason replied that he was glad I had come to him, that he wanted to know what was troubling me so that he could make me more comfortable, and that he was willing to help in any way he could.

I began by laying a background, to give him a context so that, I hoped, he would understand where I was coming from. I conveyed my appreciation for how helpful and welcoming he and his wife had been to me by helping me settle in and adjust to life in Buffalo with their family and community. I mentioned that I had always hoped to have a positive comfortable relationship with my in-laws. I truly enjoyed being with his family, I said, and hoped that my relationship with them would grow closer over time. Jason replied that the sentiments were mutual.

It was now time to get to the point. "Well," I began, "we all know that I come from a very different background from you and Wil." Jason agreed that our differences were on the cultural level, although they were not necessarily negative. "And I don't believe," I continued, "that it's fair to pass judgment on people before you understand the context and experiences that have shaped them." Jason heartily agreed. "So," I said, "I would hate for you to think I'm passing judgment on you. Rather, I just want to clear up some things that are creating tension for me and preventing me from feeling more at home here." Jason said he sincerely understood. I then chose my words very carefully, speaking slowly, which is not my usual style. "It has to do with what *I* (putting my hand on my chest for emphasis) have been raised to consider racism."

There was recognition in his eyes and his voice as he said, "Oh, I see. . . ." He knew what I meant and I felt relieved. He acknowledged the tension we both felt on the occasions when I openly disagreed with him on these matters. I said, "I understand that your opinions have been shaped by your own experiences. But I have to tell you what it's like for me, coming from a completely different world." I explained the atmosphere in which I was raised and educated. I told him my views and how I believe I have come to hold them. I told him that some of the people I most care about fall into the categories he criticizes so often. "So you see," I went on, "I know you never intended to insult me personally, but you know how you hate it when people bust on your best friend Roger, for wearing flannel shirts and work boots? Well, it's the same thing for me. When you bust on gays, you're busting on my good friend Sally, and so it feels like you're busting on me."

I could see by Jason's face that he was truly affected by this comment. He told me that he had never considered this before, but that my explanation had cast a different light on his views. I had known before how highly Jason valued his friendships and how loyal he was to his family and friends. Therefore, I had hoped that expressing my point in that way would draw some empathy from him rather than defensiveness. I now saw that I had been right on target. Jason explained that he's never taken prejudice personally because all of his friendships and other important connections had been with people very similar to himself. He said that his views were a result of being from a small, rural, homogeneous home town, and from the values he had learned from his family. I told him that I didn't expect him to change his views. All I wanted was for him to respect my views and background. I knew that I couldn't force him to stop saying words and making comments that offend me. But I did convey to him very clearly and calmly that those remarks disturbed me, and made me so uncomfortable that they severely impeded any trust that could develop between us. I reiterated that my relationship with him was very important to me, but gave him a clear message that his remarks would prevent us from growing any closer.

He said that he genuinely understood, and that he never wanted to make me feel uncomfortable. It seemed that he had truly never before considered that his attitudes would evoke such negative responses from people who were not members of the groups he insulted. He told me that he respected me tremendously for confronting him on this issue. It seemed that I was the first person who had talked about it with him in this way. Other people, including Wil, had disagreed with him, but only gave up frustrated and intimidated by his defensive responses. In the past, Jason had always expressed his prejudice as though he was certain that he was right. People who knew him, including Wil, had always commented and joked about how opinionated Jason was, how impossible it was to change his views on anything. Yet here he was sitting across from me, his face and posture softer than I had ever seen them, telling me that I had opened up a whole new way of thinking for him.

Jason told me he couldn't promise that he would become completely non-racist or "pro-gay," especially overnight. But he recognized now how I felt and would make every conscious effort to not express his prejudice in front of me.

I replied that this was all I was really asking for, and stressed how much I appreciated his understanding. I realized that Jason truly cared about my impression of him. He didn't want me to think poorly of him. Once I saw how open he was to my feedback, I realized how unfair I had been by not giving him a chance all this time, and I even confided this to him. Interestingly, I saw that while other people may have been afraid to confront him, he had felt alienated, not empowered, because of the distance their fear had created. He was so appreciative of my confrontation because I was sharing myself with him and telling him how he could help, without insulting his character. I think this is what he meant when he told me, with emotion in his voice, "You have to know, Laura, that no one has ever talked to me like this before. I really appreciate this."

Jason and I talked for almost four hours that evening. We learned a lot about each other's background and perspectives. We broke down many barriers and connected more than we ever had up until that point. I still did not agree with some of his perspectives. I was impressed and appreciative that he had been so open to my position and so willing to change his behavior in my presence. Yet his responsiveness to me did not stop me from holding him accountable for the development of his own belief system. I still hold him responsible for his tendencies to stereotype people, both in the past and after our talk. I will never be satisfied with the excuse that a person is prejudiced because he or she comes from a small homogeneous town. I believe there are more individual, intrapersonal reasons why we choose to accept and maintain intolerant attitudes. Although we may be shaped by past experiences and circumstances, we also play a part in choosing our experiences and in how we interpret them.

At the time of our talk, Jason had lived away from his hometown for several years. Yet instead of allowing this time in a major city to open his mind, he had used this exposure to further solidify his earlier beliefs.

To be honest, this aspect of Jason still disturbs me and causes me to be somewhat wary of him. Yet I know that if I had simply confronted him with this particular issue, I would have gotten a defensive response. As strong as my opinions may be, it would not serve my purpose to attack Jason's character. As much as I wish he were different in this area, it would be inappropriate of me to make it my project to transform him by directly criticizing him. My goal in that conversation was real-istic. I only expected him to listen to my position and respect my feelings enough to stop making prejudiced comments when we were together. I was able to accomplish this goal because I began by sharing my side with him and then explain-ing in a non-judgmental way how I was affected by his com-ments. The fact that he did allow his mind to be opened by what I said, and the fact that his attitudes began to shift as a result is because of who he is, and for this I give him credit and respect, as well as my appreciation. I truly love this aspect of Jason.

I know that we all hold intolerant attitudes because of our own personal insecurities. I probably reacted so strongly to Jason partly because I identify with him. He expresses his intolerance differently than I do, but the mechanisms behind his attitudes probably strike a chord with me, thus making me uncomfortable. My own tendency is to immediately react to him instead of looking inside myself and asking what is hap-pening for me at that moment, what is coming up for me. I have to pay attention to this tendency and try to stay centered, although I admit this is easier said than done. Yet my point-ing a finger at Jason and calling him a racist is not so differ-ent, in this respect, from when Jason points a finger at wel-fare recipients and calls them lazy.

Our conversation had finally wound down, straying off into other tangents. The sun had set around us as we finished talking, and suddenly I realized we had been sitting in the darkness of the unlit living room for quite some time. I felt exhausted but light and content. I had made peace with myself and with Jason. We were no longer strangers to one another. It was a meaningful Passover after all.

In this example, Laura's actions coincided with each of our guidelines. She began by consciously attending to the figure-making process in the here and now while driving over to Jason's house, and she actively continued to do so throughout their conversation. She used her awareness of herself and the discomfort she was feeling to acknowledge that something important was happening between her and Jason. She recognized that focusing on the groups that Jason was targeting would obscure the process between them and that it was this process that had to be attended to; she knew she could no longer make herself a "stranger" to Jason. By taking the time to discuss their differences in private without the bustle of work activities that normally surrounded them, she allowed their discussion to progress at a slow enough pace that the pressure to prematurely join or to distance was greatly reduced. In emphasizing her own experience by talking about her definition of racism and her experience with gays and lesbians, she talked to Jason about herself and who she was at that moment. In this way she made herself what we have called a vivid individual. Furthermore, she encouraged Jason to talk about his experiences, and she listened to his stories openly, thereby enabling his differentiation in a more effective manner. She knew that she could not demand that he change his views—any change would be up to him and on his own time. Her request from him in this interaction was simply to be seen and heard, not for him to change. Yet she continued to hope he would change when she related that she still holds him accountable for his prejudices. She has done her part and hopes he will find a way to do his.

In recognizing how she had made herself a stranger to Jason by not expressing her views, Laura acknowledged to herself that she had made herself vague in her past interactions with Jason. In this conversation with Jason, Laura changed how she was perceived. She did this by talking of herself and her personal history and experiences; she used many so-called "I" statements. Simultaneously, Laura supported Jason in his self-definition, helping him to become a less judgmental individual. She did not approach him from an authoritarian perspective, and she did not ask him to introject her perspective. She did not condescend to him, nor did she allow him to condescend to her. Rather she approached him from an egalitarian stance which permitted each of them to feel and openly express the tension that arose at those times when they had openly disagreed with one another. During the conversation described in this example, Laura's motivation was to understand and be understood, to see a vivid man in Jason and to be a vivid person herself. She was successfully meeting and befriending someone who was important to her and whom she had kept at an arm's length over a fairly long period of time. She overcame her fears and anxieties that had led to her earlier poor handling and she engaged in a way that exemplifies what we have been describing as good handling.

12

Elaboration and Reflections

Throughout this book we have focused attention on particular examples of invitations to collaborate with projections and on interactions among small groups of people. As we worked with these examples and discussed our work with others, two larger themes emerged. First, we gradually became aware that it is much easier for people to remember instances when they have been the victim of a projection or when someone made them uncomfortable by issuing an invitation to collaborate than it is to remember times when they have projected onto others. In this chapter, we examine some possible reasons why this disparity exists when people recall their experiences with projections. Second, as we worked, we also became aware that projections are very common and are woven into the fabric of our everyday lives. As we reflected on the frequency of projections, we realized that even though projections are usually made by an individual person, they are not merely personal or interpersonal phenomena; they are embedded in the conventions of modern social institutions. In this chapter, we also reflect on such social conventions.

In general, it seems to us that it is easier for persons to recall instances in which they or their reference group have been the object of projecting processes than it is for them to remember when they were the persons doing the projecting. Thus, Jews find it easier to detect anti-Semitism aimed at them than to notice their own racism; and African Americans can readily list many occasions of experiencing racial discrimination, but they are less primed to see anti-white, anti-Latino, or anti–Asian-American expressions of their own racism, and when they do become aware of their bias they are commonly uneasy about it. Indeed, at one time it was popularly said that oppressed groups could not themselves be called racist since racism was a matter of power and could appear only in powerful, majority groups. This may have been a way for such persons to avoid their discomfort about being themselves discriminatory. We now want to suggest what we think about this disparity between being the object and being the subject of bias in the light of our analysis.

To experience bigotry directed at oneself or one's community is to be challenged in respect to absorbing, taking in, or introjecting what is being thrust upon one or one's in-group. Being attacked in a bigoted way is being asked to internalize the contents of that attack. One of the great problems of oppressed people is that they have been in subordinate positions of threat, and they have had to stifle themselves over and over again and, as a result of such self-conquest they introject that which is toxic to them. The commonly seen self-hatred in oppressed people stems from such social domination that has cultivated these personal introjecting propensities. The undoing of self-hatred and oppression, as argued by Fanon (1963), Freire (1970), Bulhan (1985), and Lichtenberg (1990, 1994), among others, is importantly an undoing of identification with the aggressor—developing processes that give relief from such toxic introjects.

Struggling with problematic introjects is about dealing with oneself in respect to others, with the accent on oneself. Being the object of a projection stimulates inner conflicts—conflicts between one's own spontaneous nature and the introjects that contest with this nature, which must be explored and resolved. Access to the troubles created by these problematic introjects is relatively direct since the main story is being played out within the psyche of the oppressed person. Through the internalizing of the oppressor, the dominator and the dominated have become the same individual. Liberatory endeavors succeed by again socializing the conflict and by centering the dominating force as out there in the social scene. When the oppressed person undoes an introject, he or she no longer exerts internal control in the service of a powerful other but rather struggles against currently dominating persons in the social environment.

Projecting, in contrast to introjecting, is importantly distributing an inner conflict by planting part of the conflict in the social context. Part of the emotional load of the conflict is meant to be carried by someone else, by the object of the projection. Accordingly, it is not easy to know one's projections, to have an awareness that one is right now projecting, or to recognize that the quality that is being attributed to the other is indeed a component of one's nature. The target, with whom the projecting person is delusionally fused, the most obvious element in the experience, is foreground while the projecting person's inner life is background. The event appears to be social rather than intrapersonal. The component of the projecting person that is most problematic is hidden from that person by being located elsewhere.

In short, people gag on demands for introjecting others' ideas or feelings; they experience an instinctive, strong, even physical response to such a demand. On the other hand, when people project, they remain strangely unaware of their psychic details; they experience an emptying, sometimes even a catharsis, but there is little to no awareness of what they are emptying from themselves. The social situation from the vantage point of receiving demands to introject differs dramatically from the social situation of sending out projections. Internal burdens are being added in the case of the demand for introjecting, while they are being distributed into the social situation in the case of projecting. It is this difference in the location of the burdens that leads people to remember vividly times when they were the objects of projection while forgetting times when they themselves were projecting.

This difference between demands for introjection and the sending forth of projections, both in what is experienced and what the interpersonal relations look like, gives a peculiar cast to our argument in this book. In the phenomenon we scrutinize, the invitation to collaborate with a projection, the projecting person seems to be a "subject," an agent (however unawares of his or her inner life), while the invitee who is expected to introject appears to be an "object" (full of disturbing inner experience). The projecting person is *doing* something while the invitee is *reacting* to what has happened. In our guidelines, the emphasis is directed in the opposite way: we are encouraging the invitee to claim his or her status as a "subject" in a social way, and to develop a sense of agency in an intense emotional situation. This is why we seem to be talking *to* invitees while talking *about* projecting persons. Our emphasis has been on the invitee as becoming the actor and the projecting person as the one who is to be the recipient of the action. This slant derives from the fact that the projecting person is expecting to achieve confluence prematurely by having the invitee introject his or her projection. The reactions of poor handling reflect the invitee's difficulties with healthy assertion of agency. These reactions are either blanket refusals to introject and to become fused with the projecting person, or they are indiscriminate submissions to the projecting person. The guidelines for good handling, on the other hand, can be seen as ways to meet the world with healthy introjecting tendencies, that is, carefully choosing what to take in and what to alienate, rather than either refusing to take in anything from the other or swallowing what is offered without destructuring it.

At this point, we would like to note that the invitee's sudden, spontaneous reaction to the invitation may contribute to what one person referred to as "an odor of sanctity" in our examples. When suddenly invited to collaborate, the narrators of most of our examples were "stunned," "shocked," or "astonished." Whereas these strong reactions are often seen as judgmental and the invitees as sanctimonious, if we take into consideration the disorientation that such demands for confluence and introjection create in the relationship, then we are more likely to view these strong reactions as the invitee's startled response to the sudden necessity of having to assert oneself. The "odor of sanctity" reflects that an introject has been touched or the person is awkwardly rejecting introjecting in the present.

The momentary stunned reactions can easily lead to poor handling and to righteous and indignant behavior, and the narrators of many of our examples do describe some righteous or indignant feelings at the moment at which they are invited to collaborate. Good handling consists of a choice on the part of the invitee to avoid acting upon these feelings by joining or distancing, to slow down the process, and to respond in friendship. Invitees who engage in good handling choose to move beyond the initial shock and to bring themselves fully into the relationship in an assertive but nonthreatening way.

By mastering the demands for confluence and for introjection that are contained in invitations to collaborate with a projection, an invitee is respectfully both challenging and supporting the projecting person. The challenge is to the faulty methods for creating community; the support is to the intention to community. From this challenge and support comes the intention to friendship.

When handling is good, the projecting person, in turn, experiences as less repulsive that which is being expelled by means of the projection. Consequently, he or she is more likely to become aware of what was disowned. Thus, pressures on invitees to internalize and on projecting persons to externalize are reduced by good handling; an invitee's hypersensitivity to being forced to internalize something unwanted is diminished while a projecting person's ability to tolerate self-awareness is heightened. All parties achieve a better balance in being both subject and object. Thus, the more one

participates in interactions in which good handling is taking place
(as projecting person or as invitee), the greater is the experience
of mutuality and common purpose.

   This brings us to another important point. When we have differentiated between a projecting person and an invitee, we have
constantly reminded ourselves that no one is simply one or the
other. We are all both projecting persons and invitees at one time
or another. Everyone projects a great deal in everyday life, just as
everyone is called upon to deal with projecting processes quite regularly. Similarly, when we have referred to an invitee as engaging in
good handling, we mean *this time* that person is doing so. No one is
always in the category of a good handler or a poor handler. Even
the best of good handling, as we have pointed out repeatedly,
is probably flawed as well. The building of community and the
intention to friendship are best seen, consequently, as ongoing,
unfinished efforts, endeavors that smack of the ambiguity of life
itself. Divisions of persons into projecting persons versus invitees,
or division of invitees into good handlers versus poor handlers are
divisions that very likely contain some projections themselves. Dichotomous, either/or thinking is especially congenial for projecting
processes.

   We have also been asserting that invitations to collaborate with
a projection arise in social circumstances that involve high arousal
of feelings. The projections are a function of the inability to support such a level of emotion and to express directly to those around
one what is contained in that emotion. We can now point out that
such projections are themselves a function of the mores of the group
as much as the frailties of the individual. By this we mean that most
current social conventions do not foster intense, close social emotions of the sort that lead to healthy confluence in congenial gatherings. While all kinds of intense sensations may be promoted, those
that eventuate in intimate self-disclosure and a meeting of all persons present are not fostered. In modern society, persons are not
accustomed to the feelings that accompany intimacy when we are

in small groups. Individuals have taken on the dictate that they should reserve intense encounters for private moments and for the limited occasions allocated and dedicated to the sharing of love.

Those intense moments that do occur in our current society are usually of the kind that divide one from another. For example, although there can be anger that brings people close together as well as anger that pushes them apart, in our social system we have perfected the divisive form of anger. We have done so to the point that most of us think all anger inherently separates the angry person and the object of his or her anger. Yet, as Paul Goodman (Perls et al. 1951) pointed out, "anger is a sympathetic passion, it unites persons because it is admixed with desire" (p. 344). We can develop those ways of being angry in our social settings that promote friendship, not enmity. Good enough handling of an invitation to collaborate with a projection, thus, is itself a move toward changing the mores of the groups in which we live. And that is not a simple matter.

Social conventions are norms that have been internalized and are carried out mostly unawares. Thus, the conventions are themselves introjects, and if they have been inculcated through indoctrination rather than democratic education, they are not easy to undo. This is the basic lesson of Freire's *Pedagogy of the Oppressed* (1970), a pedagogy heavily influenced by psychoanalytic thought. Early in life we learn what is acceptable intense emotional expression, both as to the intensity itself and the circumstances and forms in which various feelings are allowed free play. For instance, small children are often punished for their vital angry responses to being frustrated, and, as a result, they learn to subdue their anger, only to find it coming out in distorted forms. Similarly, direct expressions of love, of vulnerability, of curiosity, of helplessness, of sadness are not facilitated adequately in modern life such that they lead to communion. We cannot emphasize enough that all of these emotional qualities do in fact come out, but because in our social system the community has not constructed conventions that promote their direct and healthy expression in many contexts, they are mostly seen in distorted forms. For example, at work people do not customarily reveal their felt vulnerability. Seldom do family members openly talk about their feelings of helplessness. And friends often restrain themselves from expressing their love for fear that it will lead to unfortunate consequences. Yet these are the emotions that regularly arise in social gatherings. At the cookout on July Fourth, people remember but do not mention the family member who was with them last year but is now gone. People avoid speaking to each other about their fearful feelings on the economic front, even while exchanging presents for a given holiday or anniversary. At a wedding, guests are reluctant to deal with the racist remark that came out of nowhere and disturbed them greatly lest they disrupt the happy occasion. The projections we have been describing throughout the book are precisely distorted expressions of feelings that if they were more properly managed could lead to bonding and community rather than to the sense of discomfort, danger, and isolation that they regularly produce.

Jill Ker Conway in *True North* (1994) commented on social conventions that are internalized. She noticed how over the centuries social mores have determined the acceptable expression of emotions by women. In her book she reflects upon her sense that in the past many women who were activists and influential in the social world were more constrained in their private lives. For instance, the Grimke sisters in the Abolition movement and Jane Addams in this century became powerful social figures through their actions and writings yet were less dynamic and forceful in their private relationships. In studying the lives of socially influential women, Conway was struck by how common this disparity was, and she sought to explain it. Her reflections on the matter led her to conclude that the social system, generation after generation, exerted pressure for girls and women to repress more than their sexuality. Girls and women were raised to suppress all kinds of powerful and intense human feelings, to keep them not only from consciousness, but from social encounters as well. Only approved social emotions were tolerated and supported in personal encounters, and this demand for self-control, which we have referred to as self-conquest, was a significant means for creating gender identifications. She concluded that social systems operate to control what can be thought and felt and in this way they act to give structure to the psyches of both women and men. We would add to her understanding that social systems create dichotomies not only for engendering their members but also for dividing classes, races, ethnic groups, and persons of different sexual orientations.

A sophisticated Gestalt therapist, Carol Swanson (personal communication 1995), has contemplated how she continues to undo socially constructed introjects:

> I am experiencing a gradual "psychic thawing." I am beginning to see with a limited peripheral vision how pervasive this process is in my interpersonal relations. It is like viewing a watermark—I see it and then it disappears and then reappears.
>
> On our run yesterday, I was able to tell my friend Bruce (a Kansas farm boy, not unlike my father) that I am strong, competent, and also vulnerable; I often experienced him only seeing the strong side of this polarity, even when I make explicit my need. I also said, there are many times I hold back my need, and that is my difficulty. It was a risk for me to put this out. His response was: "I do not know what to say at those times." I said, with feeling, "Say that." This pattern has been ongoing for years, with Bruce and with many others. I think it is difficult if not impossible for most of us to imagine a different kind of life. Once again, I find this true in imagining that I could throw off the shackles of the responsibility and other introjects I live by.

While it is true that women have been encouraged to be emotional and vulnerable, they have not been supported in being both strong and weak, influential and vulnerable, according to the actuality of their experience of the moment. Jill Ker Conway's assessment of women's consciousness-raising groups in the early days of the recent feminist movement concerned just this issue: women could affirm their strength, gather support through their vulnerability, and not need to divide themselves such that they could be strong in the service of someone else and quite weak in representing themselves. These consciousness-raising endeavors were what we are here calling efforts to change the mores that guide everyday life.

We believe that, like these women participating in consciousness-raising groups, many of us have introjected the mores of society at an early age. Unfortunately, as adults, we often don't realize that the real power differences that affected us as children are no longer in existence between ourselves and others. Yet we continue to respond to the world as though we are relatively helpless and unable to exert strong influence except possibly with children and others who are visibly vulnerable. As adults we are more capable of taking care of ourselves, yet we continue to restrict our living space by remaining within the boundaries established much earlier in our lives. We exaggerate the power of others and minimize our own influence.

Part of the difficulty in breaking out of the social conventions that restrict us is a pressure to conform and the shaming that generally accompanies this pressure. When we react strongly in social situations, we are often labeled as being "unstable," "volatile," or just "too emotional." In their groups the women in consciousness-raising activities learned that they could be intense while keeping contact with others, and they were not denigrated for their intensity and their vulnerability. They discovered that they could speak their individuality and find that they were not only understood and accepted, but that they were speaking the truth of women more generally. They could be vivid individuals and then could merge with others who had had similar backgrounds and similar ways of accommodating. From this learning, they generalized that the personal is political.

Jill Ker Conway's contrasting how a woman could be powerful on the political scene and weak and "romantic" in the personal sphere, and her connecting this to women's consciousness-raising groups brings us back to our beginning. The relation of the small interaction to the larger social and political strife, of hearing a sexist remark and handling it poorly as the ground for the acceptance of large-scale sexism in the discrimination against women, has been our preoccupation from the start. Now we believe that we have learned something from the theory of good enough handling in small groups that is applicable to the large social scene, too. We do not mean to take away from our focus on handling in the social gathering. Indeed, we want to acknowledge again how important we think such endeavors are. What we do wish to note, however, is another contribution to political life.

We have suggested that the projections embodied in racism, classism, sexism, homophobia, and so on, come from profound self-hatred, which in turn derives from introjections. Group solidarity, as Freud pointed out long ago in *Group Psychology and the Analysis of the Ego* (1921), is based on processes of identification, which are processes based on introjection. Women learning what it is to be womanly, Asian-Americans learning what it is to be Asian-American, Catholics learning what it is to be Catholic, are all instances of customs being inculcated by teachings and rewards and punishments that promote identification with the group. In-groups are essentially groups with common identifications.

How these identifications are established is the crucial issue in whether they shall lead to in-group animosities toward out-groups or whether they shall lead to group solidarity without such enmities. It is here that our analysis of good enough handling makes its contribution. Those identifications that do not foster self-hatred and do not lead to in-group–out-group animosities result from communion that happens after individuals assert their unique being in the contact and withdrawal cycle. These identifications come from healthy group loyalty because self-enhancement is encouraged and self-definition is supported and all members of the group are represented in the collective achievements. Conversely, those identifications that are based on introjections that take place when premature confluence is required, which is the case in dominating child-rearing, in authoritarian education, and in indoctrinating religion, are identifications that promote rivalry and conflict between larger groups.

We can contrast mass rallies during the time of Hitler with the Million Man March in the United States in 1995. In the Nazi era the rallies caused the individuals assembled to be submerged in the larger group; in the Million Man March, the participants came from their diverse and individuated places, and judged the leaders according to how they, the participants, were met. The identifications in the two different rallies were profoundly different precisely in the dimension that we have specified. The question must always be asked: Does the larger group demand of its members that they submerge themselves as the price of membership or does it promote the merging of vivid, separate individuals? The answer to that question determines whether the larger group (religious, gender, racial, sexual orientation, class) can be expected to rely on intergroup conflict for its solidarity. At bottom, groups that function in democratic ways will contrast with groups that function in authoritarian ways according to the processes of contact and withdrawal that characterize interpersonal interactions as well as mass-based interactions. Democracy does indeed begin in town meetings, in the labor hall, and in conversations at social gatherings.

We believe there is much more space than people customarily recognize in local social interactions to change the mores and to create history. To experiment with one's social relations with awareness that one is making a new world can be both liberating and enlivening. We suspect that invitees tend to exaggerate the social norms that prohibit intensity of feelings that surface in good handling, and, consequently, they exert excessive self-control. Most people subdue themselves when they might risk themselves by encountering projecting persons. Anticipation of shame plays a large role in this self-limiting process. Plunging ahead alone into unexplored emotional territory threatens the individual with getting lost, and it is often the separateness that makes such people prime targets for shaming and the felt isolation that makes one so vulnerable to the effects of this shaming. By paying attention to the here-and-now aspects of the relationship, by describing the impact of the interaction as one presently experiences it, and by encouraging the other to describe his or her real experience, present and past, an individual can avoid such separation and isolation. Through shared explorations, persons can create relationships that are satisfying, intense, and respectful. Despite the limiting social mores, they can say to one another, "This is where we meet and we can continue to negotiate the boundaries of these meetings as we become more curious about one another and more open to one another."

It is important to remember that the deep emotional experience that accompanies good handling brings an intensity to social gatherings that can be welcomed rather than shaming. We know that sometimes people at a party gravitate toward the room in the house where the heated political discussion is taking place or where the emotional travails of a family member or friend are aired. Our examples, too, show that good enough handling is gratifying to all involved. Not only Laura, but also Jason was enlivened; not only the Weissers, but also Trapp; not only Joan, but also Tamika; and so on.

We remind the reader that there is no "innocence" in a social gathering when a racist, sexist, homophobic, or classist remark is dropped in the conversation. Once an individual is put in the situation as an observer, and thus an invitee of such remarks, that person must handle it one way or another. In this respect we become responsible for what we hear. We can only choose how we will handle such invitations to collaborate with a projection.

We caution the responsive reader that he or she will probably not do things well most of the time, especially early on in experimenting with what we have proposed. These matters are highly charged, arouse great feeling, and differ in intensity from customary social discourse. Much comes up in all the parties when issues of racism, sexism, homophobia, or class differences are foreground and are used as expressions of projecting tendencies. Even those professionals who have dealt with projections many times in their practices are not always highly skilled in this regard, especially out of their offices and in social gatherings. So we ask the reader to be self-indulgent, self-forgiving, and self-rewarding along the way. Merely trying is a first step. Applying the guidelines will help, as we know from persons who have already been influenced by these ideas and have reported back to us on their efforts.

Finally, we want to say that we are not implying that good handling of invitations to collaborate with a projection in a social gathering will itself change the world. We know the difference between interpersonal relations and large social movements. We do mean to say, however, that unless this work is also done, people will not know how to go about the processes of changing the world. We believe that good handling in the small-scale social world enables effective acting in the large-scale endeavors. At a minimum, one can see more clearly the principles of social systems that foster rivalry and hatred and those that promote friendship, respect, and community. Acting well in one's small social circle is also making history and in some small degree changing the world.

Appendix: Guidelines for Befriending Projecting Persons

In the text we have discussed at length our guidelines for good enough handling. Here we present an outline of these guidelines and the main themes we have developed.

I. Attend to the figure-making process in the here and now.
   A. Be prepared and willing to engage in a lively encounter, to make the transaction an interesting one.
      1. You may have to bypass norms that inhibit this liveliness (e.g., at parties).
      2. Be aware that you are in the presence of an arousal or excitement that is felt to be hard to experience directly.
   B. Pay attention to the current process instead of focusing on the content of the projection; talk *to* the other rather than *about* the out-group that is not present.
   C. Slow down the process, keeping it in the figure-forming or negotiating phase.
   D. Make the transaction safe by increasing support, decreasing arousal, or both.
      1. Be able to find ways to support the projecting person and yourself without supporting the projection itself.

2. Remember that no effort will be fully "good handling." Accept the limitations of your effort as well as small gains while tolerating the ambivalence and ambiguity of your efforts.

E. Be focused on meeting the other rather than trying to change him or her; you cannot make another person change; you can only foster conditions that promote change.

II. Become a vivid individual in the transaction without demanding premature confluence and without distancing or withdrawing from the projecting person.

A. Intend to meet the other as a friend and an equal.

1. Do not patronize, be superior, or know too much too soon.

2. Be aware that your perception of a projection happening is an hypothesis or hunch.

3. Be sincerely curious and open to the other.

B. Be able to openly describe and acknowledge your experience.

1. You may have some common ground with the projecting person which is hard for you to own.

2. You may need to make yourself vulnerable even in the presence of persons who have trouble with "weakness" and vulnerability. You can be both vulnerable and aware of your own strength and influence.

III. Support the projecting person in creating self-definition without giving in to premature confluence in the figure-forming process.

A. Be interested in and foster open acknowledgment of the projecting person's experiences.

1. Be aware that all projections are based on some truth and that sincere interest in that truth is important to meeting the other.

    2. You may need to prepare yourself to acknowledge negatives that characterize the out-group.

    3. Your interest here is on expanding awareness.

B. Search for the story of the projecting person in a way to soften and ameliorate his or her self-hatred.

C. Be willing to risk affiliation or overlap with one who is ideologically different from yourself; be able to tolerate temporary connection with someone or something that is alien to you.

References

Angyal, A. (1965). *Neurosis and Treatment: A Holistic Theory*, ed. E. Hanfman and R. M. Jones. New York: Wiley.

Bion, W. R. (1970). *Attention and Interpretation: A Scientific Approach to Insight in Psycho-Analysis and Groups*. New York: Basic Books.

Bulhan, H. A. (1985). *Frantz Fanon and the Psychology of Oppression*. New York: Plenum.

Catherall, D. R. (1991). Aggression and projective identification in the treatment of victims. *Psychotherapy* 28:145–149.

Conway, J. K. (1994). *True North: A Memoir*. New York: Knopf.

Dicks, H. V. (1967). *Marital Tensions*. New York: Basic Books.

Fanon, F. (1963). *The Wretched of the Earth*. New York: Grove.

Fenichel, O. (1945). *The Psychoanalytic Theory of Neurosis*. New York: Norton.

Freire, P. (1970). *Pedagogy of the Oppressed*. New York: Herder & Herder.

Freud, S. (1911). Psycho-analytic notes on an autobiographical account of a case of paranoia (dementia paranoides). *Standard Edition* 12:9–82.

——— (1921). Group psychology and the analysis of the ego. *Standard Edition* 18:67–143.

Funderburg, L. (1994). *Black, White, Other: Biracial Americans Talk about Race and Identity*. New York: Morrow.

Gemmill, G. (1986). The dynamics of the group shadow in inter-group relations. *Small Group Behavior* 17:229–239.

Gibbons, D., Lichtenberg, P., and van Beusekom, J. (1994). Working with victims: being empathic helpers. *Clinical Social Work Journal* 22:211–222.

Hamilton, N. G. (1990). The containing function of the analyst's projective identification. *International Journal of Psycho-Analysis* 71:445–453.

Hooks, B. (1994). *Teaching to Transgress: Education as the Practice of Freedom.* New York: Routledge.

Klein, M. (1946). Notes on some schizoid mechanisms. *International Journal of Psycho-Analysis* 27:99–110.

Kovel, J. (1992). Naming and conquest. *Monthly Review* 44:49–60.

Laplanche, J., and Pontalis, J. B. (1973). *The Language of Psycho-Analysis,* trans. D. S. Smith. New York: Norton.

Lichtenberg, P. (1987). Attachment and the brightening and dimming of self. In *The Book of the Self: Person, Pretext, and Process,* ed. P. Young-Eisendrath and J. Hall, pp. 331–341. New York: New York University Press.

———— (1990). *Undoing the Clinch of Oppression.* New York: Peter Lang.

———— (1991). Intimacy as a function of autonomy and merging. *The Gestalt Journal* 14:27–43.

———— (1994). *Community and Confluence: Undoing the Clinch of Oppression* (*2nd ed.*). Cleveland, OH: Gestalt Institute of Cleveland Press.

Macmurray, J. (1957). *The Self as Agent.* London: Faber and Faber.

Meissner, W. W. (1980). A note on projective identification. *Journal of the American Psychoanalytic Association* 28:43–67.

Morrison, A. (1986). On projective identification in couples groups. *International Journal of Group Psychotherapy* 36:55–72.

Ogden, T. H. (1979). On projective identification. *International Journal of Psycho-Analysis* 60:357–373.

Perls, F., Hefferline, R., and Goodman, P. (1951). *Gestalt Therapy: Excitement and Growth in the Human Personality.* New York: Julian Press.

Polster, E., and Polster, M. (1973). *Gestalt Therapy Integrated.* New York: Brunner/Mazel.

Staub, E. (1985). The psychology of perpetrators and bystanders. *Political Psychology* 6:61–85.

Watterson, K. (1995). *Not by the Sword: How the Love of a Cantor and His Family Transformed a Klansman.* New York: Simon & Schuster.

Index

About the Authors

Philip Lichtenberg, Ph.D., is the Mary Hale Chase Professor in Social Sciences and Social Work and Social Research at the Graduate School of Social Work and Social Research, Bryn Mawr College, where he has been teaching for thirty-five years. He is also Co-Director of the Gestalt Therapy Institute of Philadelphia. He maintains a psychotherapy practice.

Janneke Maria van Beusekom, Ph.D., is in the private practice of psychotherapy at Life Management Associates in Lancaster, Pennsylvania. Formerly an assistant professor in economics, she is a graduate of Bryn Mawr's School of Social Work and Social Research.

Dorothy Gibbons, M.A., M.S.S., is a Geriatric Mental Health Clinician for Intercommunity Action, Inc. in Philadelphia. She is a recent graduate of the Gestalt Therapy Institute of Philadelphia and is currently involved in training in the Agazarian Approach to Systems-Centered Group-as-a-Whole Therapy.